Jennifer Chiaverini

Harriet's Journey
from Elm Creek Quilts

100 Sampler Blocks Inspired by the Best-Selling Novel *Circle of Quilters*

 C&T PUBLISHING

Publisher: Amy Barrett-Daffin

Creative Director: Gailen Runge

Acquisitions Editor: Roxane Cerda

Managing Editor: Liz Aneloski

Editor: Beth Baumgartel

Technical Editor: Helen Frost

Cover/Book Designer: April Mostek

Production Coordinator: Zinnia Heinzmann

Production Editor: Alice Mace Nakanishi

Illustrator: Kirstie L. Pettersen

Photo Assistants: Kaeley Hammond and Lauren Herberg

Photography by Estefany Gonzalez of C&T Publishing, Inc.,
unless otherwise noted

Library of Congress Cataloging-in-Publication Data

Names: Chiaverini, Jennifer, author. | Chiaverini, Jennifer.
Circle of quilters.

Title: Harriet's journey from Elm Creek quilts : 100 sampler blocks
inspired by the best-selling novel Circle of quilters / Jennifer Chiaverini.

Description: Lafayette, CA : C&T Publishing, [2020]

Identifiers: LCCN 2020026686 | ISBN 9781617456923 (trade paperback)
| ISBN 9781617456930 (ebook)

Subjects: LCSH: Patchwork--Patterns. | Quilting--Patterns. |
Patchwork quilts.

Classification: LCC TT835 .C4535 2020 | DDC 746.46/041--dc23

LC record available at https://lccn.loc.gov/2020026686

Printed in the USA

10 9 8 7 6 5 4 3 2 1

Dedication

To readers and quilters around the world whose love for *Circle of Quilters* and the other novels in the Elm Creek Quilts series inspired this book.

Acknowledgments

I am grateful to Geraldine Neidenbach and Shelley Stevens for their extensive and patient pattern testing and editing, and to Sue Vollbrecht for her beautiful quilting. Thanks to Geraldine, Shelley, Cecile Flegg, Dana Larson Mosling, Heather Neidenbach, and Cassandra Slocum for making beautiful samplers inspired by *Harriet's Journey* for the Gallery. This book would not have been possible without the contributions of the wonderful creative team at C&T Publishing, especially Roxane Cerda, Liz Aneloski, Beth Baumgartel, Helen Frost, April Mostek, Zinnia Heinzmann, Alice Mace Nakanishi, Kirstie L. Pettersen, and Estefany Gonzalez. Many thanks to you all. Much love and gratitude to my husband, Marty, and our sons, Nicholas and Michael, for their steadfast love and encouragement. You make anything possible and everything worthwhile!

 # Contents

MORNING STAR
Block F-6   52

MRS. BRYAN'S CHOICE
Block F-7   53

NIGHT AND DAY
Block F-8   53

NINE-PATCH FRAME
Block F-9   54

NOON AND NIGHT
Block F-10   54

NORTHUMBERLAND STAR
Block G-1   55

OLD FAVORITE
Block G-2   55

OREGON CITY
Block G-3   56

OREGON TRAIL
Block G-4   57

OVERLAND STAR
Block G-5   57

PATH THROUGH THE WOODS
Block G-6   58

PENNSYLVANIA
Block G-7   58

POINSETTIA
Block G-8   59

PRAIRIE FLOWER
Block G-9   60

PRAIRIE STAR
Block G-10   61

PRICKLY POPPY
Block H-1   61

QUATREFOIL
Block H-2   62

RIBBON STAR
Block H-3   63

RISING STAR
Block H-4   63

ROCKY ROAD TO SALEM
Block H-5   64

ROYAL CROSS
Block H-6   65

SAINT LOUIS STAR
Block H-7   65

SALEM
Block H-8   66

SAWMILL
Block H-9   67

SCOTCH SQUARES
Block H-10   67

SODA SPRINGS
Block I-1   68

WHIG ROSE
Block I-2   69

SONOMA ROSE
Block I-3   70

SPINNING WHEEL
Block I-4   70

STARS AND PINWHEELS
Block I-5   71

Introduction

Maggie's Journey with Harriet from *Circle of Quilters*

Two Quilters, Separated in Time, United by an Extraordinary Sampler

In my ninth Elm Creek Quilts novel, *Circle of Quilters*, Sylvia Bergstrom Compson, Sarah McClure, and their colleagues face an unexpected conundrum when two founding Elm Creek Quilters decide to pursue other career opportunities. Who, they wonder, could possibly take their dear friends' places on the faculty at Elm Creek Quilt Camp? An Elm Creek Quilter must not only possess mastery of the quilting arts, but teaching experience, a sense of humor, and that intangible quality that allows an individual to work harmoniously within a group. Confident that the ideal quilters are just waiting to be discovered, Sarah announces an open call for applicants.

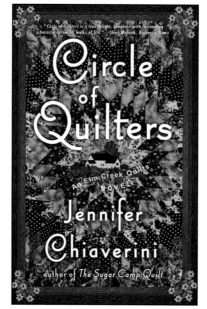

Immediately thereafter, quilters from around the country begin vying for one of the prestigious posts. Among them is Maggie Flynn, an accomplished quilter from Sacramento, California, whose discovery of an exquisite sampler quilt had utterly changed her fate.

When Maggie first spotted the quilt at a garage sale, it was in such poor condition that only upon closer examination did she realize she had stumbled upon an overlooked masterpiece. For one thing, it was absolutely filthy; a good shake flung up a cloud of dust but left the surface as grimy as before. The focus fabrics were pretty but faded, and the plain background fabric might have been white once but had discolored with age and neglect.

Chagrined, the garage sale host apologized for the quilt's condition and explained that it had been left in the garage since her family had moved to the neighborhood twenty-six years before. Her mother-in-law had purchased it at an estate auction, and when she had grown tired of it, she had given it to her son to keep dog hair off the car seats when he took his German shepherds to the park. The old quilt wasn't even really part of the sale, as they were only using it to hide an

ugly table. When she offered to part with it for five dollars, Maggie quickly accepted.

After Maggie took the quilt home, carefully spread it upon her living room floor, and studied it more closely, her initial hopes that she had discovered something very special were confirmed. The two quilts she had made years before—one a Girl Scout badge requirement, the other a gift for her sister's firstborn—by no means made her an expert, but she knew at once that this quilt was unique, a sampler of one hundred different blocks, each six inches square and arranged in ten rows of ten. The geometric patterns of the blocks were striking, and despite its careless treatment, the quilt was free of holes, tears, and stains.

Suddenly, another astonishing discovery made Maggie gasp aloud: Along one edge, embroidered in thread that had faded to pale brown barely distinguishable from the background fabric, were the words "Harriet Findley Birch. Lowell, Mass. to Salem, Ore. 1854."

Surely this was an important clue about the quilt's provenance.

Curiosity compelled her to consult a very special team of experts—the Courtyard Quilters, a quilting bee for residents of the retirement community where Maggie worked. The ladies marveled over the long-neglected treasure, identified many of the sampler blocks, and urged Maggie to contact a museum curator and quilt artist—Grace Daniels, whom longtime readers will remember from her first series appearance in *The Cross-Country Quilters*—for advice about how to properly clean and care for the quilt. When Maggie confessed that she longed to know who Harriet Findley Birch was and what had inspired her master-piece, the Courtyard Quilters encouraged her to begin her search at the local university's archives.

Maggie entrusted Harriet's sampler to Grace for cleaning and study, and then plunged into her research project. By the time Grace returned the quilt to her, so beautifully restored that Maggie almost didn't recognize it, she had learned that Harriet Findley had been born in 1830 in rural Massachusetts, she had moved to Lowell to work in the cotton mills in 1847, and she had married Franklin Birch in 1850. Soon thereafter the couple had traveled west along the Oregon Trail and had settled in Oregon, where they had raised six children.

Maggie was struck by an exciting and yet disconcerting thought: Perhaps some of Harriet's descendants still lived in the region. The more she understood how rare and precious the quilt was, the more she realized she ought to return it to Harriet's family, if she could find them.

And yet, perhaps she could keep it too, in a sense, by painstakingly creating a replica.

She bought colored pencils, graph paper, and a ruler and began drafting the beloved little blocks, imagining Harriet Findley Birch sketching the originals so long ago. Maggie named some of the unidentified blocks after locations on the Oregon Trail—Independence Rock, Fort Bridger, Star Valley—while other titles such as Lowell Crossroads and City of Spindles were inspired by Harriet's years as a mill girl. After Maggie had completed several drawings, she visited the Courtyard Quilters' favorite quilt shop to purchase fabrics, thread,

and notions. As the months passed, she stitched blocks, drew more patterns, and visited the Goose Tracks Quilt Shop so frequently that she became good friends with the owner and several regular customers. They marveled over Harriet's sampler, and they so admired Maggie's reproduction—which she called *My Journey with Harriet*—that the shop owner hired her to teach a class, so other quilters could make their own versions. Her first class was such a success that a second promptly followed, and then another, until Maggie's classes became fixtures of the store's curriculum.

All the while, as the months passed and turned into years, Maggie continued to research Harriet Findley Birch's life. Over time, she learned that Harriet had worked as a mill girl in Lowell, Massachusetts until she married. When her husband resolved to move West, Harriet consented, though her heart broke to part from her dear friends, many of whom still worked at the mills. Knowing she would no longer be able to trade patterns with her friends, she stitched her masterwork as a record of all the blocks they knew, so that no matter how far

west she traveled, she would have a wonderful variety of patterns to choose from when making quilts for her growing family in the years to come. Scraps she had saved from her own days in the mill intermingled with pieces shared by beloved friends and relatives. Since it would have been almost impossible to sew on the seat of a jolting wagon as they crossed the country on the Oregon Trail, Harriet had pieced the blocks in Lowell and had assembled and quilted the top in Salem, Oregon. Into the quilt she had stitched her grief, her hopes, her faithfulness, and her memories, or so Maggie believed.

Maggie's popularity as a teacher—not only at Goose Tracks but at quilt guilds throughout the West Coast—inspired her to publish a *Harriet's Journey* pattern book, which became a bestseller and went into multiple editions. She longed to devote herself to quilting and teaching full-time, and when she learned of the opening on the faculty of Elm Creek Quilt Camp, it seemed like the perfect opportunity. Fortunately, the Elm Creek Quilters thought Maggie would fit perfectly into their circle of quilters, and after an interview at Elm Creek Manor, they invited her to join them.

As my longtime readers know, and as my previous six pattern books from C&T Publishing will attest, I enjoy making the quilts featured in my novels. Like Maggie, I drew the patterns for *Harriet's Journey* and wrote the instructions for each of these one hundred traditional and original blocks, although I prefer the computer rather than Maggie's colored pencils and graph paper.

If the story of Maggie, Harriet, and the Elm Creek Quilters has captured your imagination, I hope you'll enjoy making your own version of *Harriet's Journey*. The one hundred 6″ (finished) blocks you'll find within these pages are the same size as those in *Sylvia's Bridal Sampler* and *The Loyal Union Sampler*, so you can swap favorite blocks between the three quilts to create a wonderful new sampler of your own. I hope you'll find your time with *Harriet's Journey* enjoyable and worthwhile, and that you'll proudly share your creative endeavors with your own circle of quilters.

Harriet's Journey

THE QUILT

FINISHED QUILT: 90″ × 90″ • FINISHED BLOCK: 6″ × 6″ • NUMBER OF BLOCKS: 100

FABRIC REQUIREMENTS

These figures are approximations, based on fabric with 42″ usable width. Yardage amounts will vary based on your fabric choices for each individual block. For variety, I used 2 red prints and 2 gold prints instead of just one of each.

Light beige: 8 yards (includes sashing and inner border)

Dark blue: 3 yards

Medium blue: 3 yards

Red: 2 yards total

Pink: 2 yards

Medium green: 3 yards

Light green: 1 yard

Gold: 2 yards total

Multicolor floral: 4 yards (for outer border and binding)

Batting: 106″ × 106″

Backing: 9 yards

HARRIET'S JOURNEY Machine pieced and appliquéd by Jennifer Chiaverini, machine quilted by Sue Vollbrecht, 2019, Wisconsin, USA. The "Lucy's Collection" fabrics by Jennifer Chiaverini used in this quilt were provided by Red Rooster Fabrics.

The Blocks

The blocks are coded with a letter for the row and a number for the column in which the block is located (see the quilt assembly diagram, page 85). If you want to create a quilt exactly like Harriet's Journey, *place your blocks according to their grid indicators.*

Air Castle ❧ BLOCK A-1

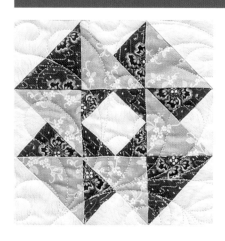

1. From light beige fabric:

• Cut 1 square 2½″ × 2½″ (A).

• Cut 2 squares 2⅞″ × 2⅞″ (C).

• Cut 1 square 3¼″ × 3¼″. Cut the square in half diagonally twice to make 4 D triangles.

2. From medium blue fabric:

• Cut 3 squares 2⅞″ × 2⅞″ (C). Cut 2 of the C squares in half diagonally once to make 4 E triangles.

3. From red fabric:

• Cut 4 squares 1½″ × 1½″ (B).

• Cut 1 square 2⅞″ × 2⅞″ (C).

• Cut 1 square 3¼″ × 3¼″. Cut the square in half diagonally twice to make 4 D triangles.

4. *Quick-Pieced Square-On-Point Units:* Make 1 quick-pieced square-on-point unit.

   a. Draw a diagonal line from corner to corner on the wrong side of each red B square.

   b. Matching one corner and aligning adjacent sides, place a red B square on a light beige A square, right sides facing.

   c. Sew on the drawn line.

   d. Trim fabric ¼″ away from the sewn line. Press the seam toward the red fabric.

   e. Repeat Steps b–d with a second red B square in the opposite corner.

   f. Repeat Steps b–d with 2 additional red B squares in the remaining corners.

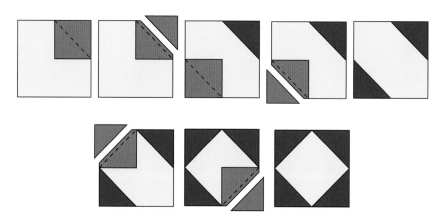

NOTE: If you prefer, use the B-3: Christmas Eve foundation paper piecing pattern C (page 97) instead. Adapt colors and adjust your fabric cutting accordingly.

5. *Quick-Pieced Half-Square Triangle (HST) Units:* Make 2 quick-pieced HST units.

   a. Draw a diagonal line from corner to corner on the wrong side of a light beige C square.

   b. Pair a light beige C square with a medium blue C square, right sides facing. Sew ¼″ on both sides of the drawn line.

c. Cut on the solid line to make 2 HST units. Press toward the medium blue fabric.

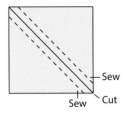

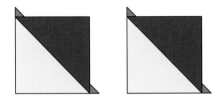

6. Repeat Step 5 with the remaining light beige C square and the red C square to make 2 HST units.

7. Noting correct color placement, sew 1 light beige D triangle to each red D triangle along the short edge. Press toward the red fabric. Make 2 D/D and 2 mirror-image D/D triangle pairs.

8. Sew 1 medium blue E triangle to each D/D and mirror-image D/D triangle pair. Press toward the medium blue fabric.

9. Noting correct color placement, sew the 2 D/D/E units to opposite sides of the square-on-point unit to make the center row. Press.

10. Noting correct color placement, sew 1 red/light beige HST unit and 1 medium blue/light beige HST unit to opposite sides of the D/D/E mirror-image units to make the top row. Press. Repeat to make the bottom row.

11. Sew the 3 rows together. Press.

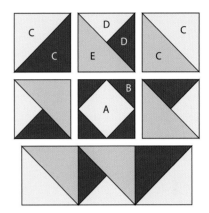

Arrowheads ❀ BLOCK A-2

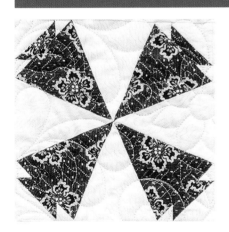

Foundation pattern A is on page 95.

1. Using light beige and dark blue fabrics, make 4 of foundation paper piecing pattern A. Press.

2. Sew the foundations into pairs to make 2 block halves. Press.

3. Sew the block halves together. Press.

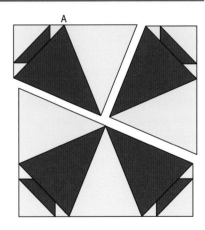

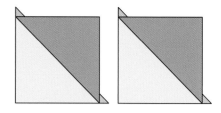

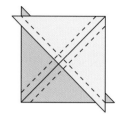

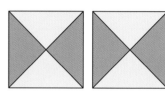

1. From medium green fabric, cut 5 squares 2½″ × 2½″ (A).

2. From light beige fabric, cut 20 squares 1½″ × 1½″ (B) and 2 squares 3¼″ × 3¼″ (C).

3. From pink fabric, cut 2 squares 3¼″ × 3¼″ (C).

4. Refer to Quick-Pieced Square-On-Point Units (page 14, Air Castle, Step 4) to make 5 quick-pieced square-on-point units with the medium green A squares and the light beige B squares.

NOTE: If you prefer, use the B-3: Christmas Eve foundation paper piecing pattern C (page 97) instead. Adapt colors and adjust your fabric cutting accordingly.

5. *Quick-Pieced Quarter-Square Triangle (QST) Units:* Make 4 quick-pieced quarter-square triangle units:

a. Draw a diagonal line from corner to corner on the wrong side of a light beige C square.

b. Pair a light beige C square with a pink C square, right sides facing. Sew ¼″ on both sides of the drawn line.

c. Cut on the solid line to make 2 HST units. Press toward the pink fabric. Repeat with the remaining pink and light beige C squares to make a total of 4 HST units.

d. On the wrong side of 1 HST unit, draw a diagonal line from a pink corner to a light beige corner.

e. Place 2 HST units together with right sides facing and pink triangles facing light beige triangles. Align edges, abut opposing seams, and pin. Sew ¼″ on both sides of the drawn line.

f. Cut on the drawn line to yield 2 QST units. Press. Repeat with the remaining HST units to make 2 more QST units.

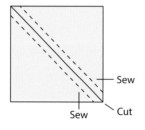

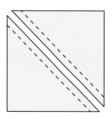

6. Sew 2 square-on-point units to opposite sides of a QST unit to make the top row. Press. Repeat to make the bottom row.

7. Sew 2 QST units to opposite sides of the remaining square-on-point unit to make the center row. Press.

8. Sew the 3 rows together. Press.

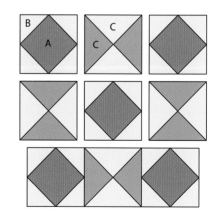

1. From light beige fabric:

• Cut 4 squares 1⅞″ × 1⅞″ (A).

• Cut 1 square 3¼″ × 3¼″. Cut the square in half diagonally twice to make 4 B triangles.

• Cut 4 rectangles 1½″ × 2½″ (C).

2. From light green fabric, cut 4 squares 1⅞″ × 1⅞″ (A) and 1 square 2½″ × 2½″ (D).

3. From dark blue fabric:

• Cut 2 squares 2⅞″ × 2⅞″. Cut each square in half diagonally once to make 4 E triangles.

• Cut 4 squares 1½″ × 1½″ (F).

4. Refer to Quick-Pieced Half-Square Triangle Units (page 14, Air Castle, Step 5) to make 8 quick-pieced HST units with the light green A squares and the light beige A squares.

5. Sew 2 light beige B triangles to opposite sides of the light green D square. Press. Sew the remaining light beige B triangles to the other sides. Press. Attach 2 dark blue E triangles to opposite sides of the unit. Press. Sew the remaining dark blue E triangles to the other sides to complete the central pieced square. Press.

6. Sew 2 HST units to the opposite ends of each light beige C rectangle. Press.

7. Sew 2 of the units created in the previous step to opposite sides of the central pieced square to create the center row. Press.

8. Sew 2 dark blue F squares to opposite ends of the remaining units. Press.

9. Sew the rows created in the previous step to the top and bottom of the center row. Press.

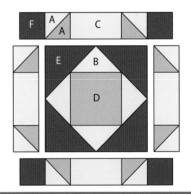

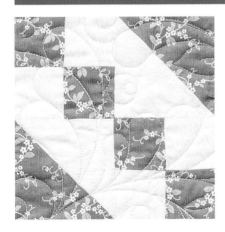

1. From light beige fabric, cut 1 square 3⅞″ × 3⅞″ (A) and 1 strip 2″ × 10″ (B).

2. From medium green fabric, cut 1 square 3⅞″ × 3⅞″ (A) and 1 strip 2″ × 10″ (B).

3. Refer to Quick-Pieced Half-Square Triangle Units (page 14, Air Castle, Step 5) to make 2 quick-pieced HST units with the medium green A squares and the light beige A squares.

4. Sew the light beige B strip to the medium green B strip lengthwise. Press toward the medium green fabric. Use a rotary cutter to crosscut the strip set into 4 strips 2″ wide.

5. Sew the strips in pairs to make 4 Four-Patch units.

6. Noting correct color placement, sew 1 Four-Patch to 1 HST unit to make the top row. Press. Repeat to make the bottom row.

7. Sew the 2 rows together. Press.

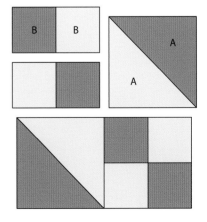

Foundation pattern B is on page 95.

1. From light beige fabric, cut 4 squares 2⅛″ × 2⅛″ (A) and 4 squares 1¾″ × 1¾″ (C).

2. From medium blue fabric, cut 4 squares 2⅛″ × 2⅛″ (A).

3. From pink fabric, cut 4 squares 1¾″ × 1¾″ (C) and 1 square 1½″ × 1½″ (D).

4. From dark blue fabric, cut 4 rectangles 1½″ × 1¾″ (E).

5. Refer to Quick-Pieced Half-Square Triangle Units (page 14, Air Castle, Step 5) to make 8 quick-pieced HST units with the light beige A squares and the medium blue A squares.

6. Make 4 of foundation paper piecing pattern B using light beige and dark blue fabrics.

7. Sew 2 pink C squares to opposite sides of a dark blue E rectangle. Press toward the dark blue fabric. Repeat to make an identical row. Sew 2 dark blue E rectangles to opposite sides of the pink D square to make the center row. Press toward the dark blue fabric. Sew the 3 rows together to make the central Nine-Patch. Press.

8. Noting correct color placement, sew 2 HST units to opposite sides of each B foundation. Press.

9. Sew 2 of the units created in the previous step to opposite sides of the central Nine-Patch to make the center row. Press.

10. Sew 2 light beige C squares to opposite ends of the remaining units to make the top row. Press. Repeat to make the bottom row.

11. Sew the 3 rows together. Press.

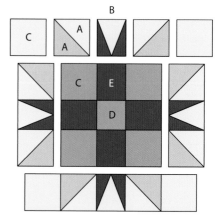

Template patterns A, C, and D are on page 95.

1. From dark blue fabric:

- Cut 4 parallelograms using template A. Flip the template over and make 4 A Reverse.

- Cut 1 square 1¼″ × 1¼″ (G).

2. From gold fabric:

- Cut 2 squares 2⅝″ × 2⅝″. Cut each square once along the diagonal to make 4 B triangles.

- Cut 4 trapezoids using template C.

3. From light beige fabric:

- Cut 4 triangles using template D. Flip the template over and make 4 D Reverse.

- Cut 6 squares 1¾″ × 1¾″. Cut each square once along the diagonal to make 12 E triangles.

- Cut 4 rectangles 1¼″ × 3⅛″ (F).

4. Sew a light beige D and D Reverse to the shortest sides of a gold C trapezoid. Press. Sew the longest side of a light beige E triangle to the longest side of the gold C trapezoid. Press. Repeat to make 4.

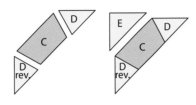

5. Sew a gold B triangle to each of the units created in the previous step. Press toward the B triangles.

6. Sewing from point to point and not into the seam allowance, sew a dark blue A parallelogram to each of the units created in the previous step. Press.

7. Using Y-seam construction, sew an A Reverse to each of the units created in the previous step. Press.

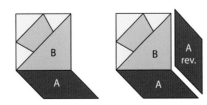

8. Sew 2 light beige E triangles to the shortest remaining sides of each A and A Reverse to make 4 block corners. Press.

9. Sew 2 block corners to opposite sides of a light beige F rectangle to create the top row. Press. Repeat to make the bottom row.

10. Sew 2 light beige F rectangles to opposite sides of the dark blue G square to make the center row. Press. Sew the 3 rows together. Press.

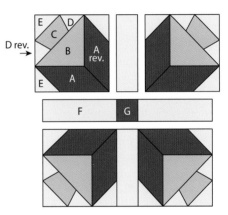

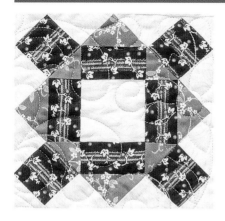

Template pattern D is on page 95.

1. From light beige fabric:

• Cut 1 square 2½″ × 2½″ (A).

• Cut 2 squares 3¼″ × 3¼″. Cut each square in half diagonally twice to make 8 B triangles.

• Cut 2 squares 1⅞″ × 1⅞″. Cut each square in half diagonally once to make 4 C triangles.

2. From medium green fabric:

• Cut 1 square 3¼″ × 3¼″. Cut the square in half diagonally twice to make 4 B triangles.

• Cut 2 squares 1⅞″ × 1⅞″. Cut each square in half diagonally once to make 4 C triangles.

3. From red fabric, cut 4 squares using template D and 4 rectangles 1½″ × 2½″ (E).

4. Sew 2 red E rectangles to opposite sides of the light beige A square. Press. Sew 2 medium green B triangles to opposite sides of the E/A/E unit. Press.

5. Sew 2 medium green C triangles to the short ends of a red E rectangle. Press. Sew a medium green B triangle to the top of the unit. Press. Repeat to make a second identical unit.

6. Sew the units created in Step 5 to opposite sides of the unit created in Step 4 to make the block center. Press.

7. Sew 2 light beige B triangles to opposite sides of a red D square. Press. Sew 1 light beige C square to the top to make 1 block corner. Press. Repeat to make a total of 4 block corners.

8. Sew 2 block corners to opposite sides of the block center. Press. Sew the 2 remaining block corners to the other sides. Press.

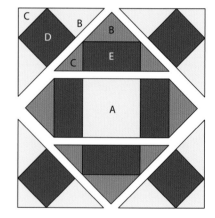

Template pattern C is on page 95.

1. From light beige fabric:

• Cut 2 squares 2⅞″ × 2⅞″. Cut each square in half diagonally to make 4 triangles (A).

• Cut 1 square 2½″ × 2½″ (B).

2. Using template C, cut 1 hexagon each from red, gold, medium green, and dark blue fabric.

3. Sewing only from point to point and not into the seam allowance, sew 2 C hexagons to opposite sides of the light beige B square. Press.

4. Using Y-seam construction and sewing in the direction of the arrows, sew the 2 remaining C hexagons to the remaining sides of the light beige B square. Press.

5. Sew the light beige A triangles to the corners of the block. Press.

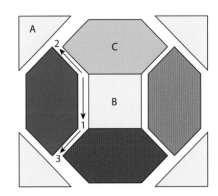

1. From dark blue fabric, cut 5 squares 2½″ × 2½″ (A).

2. From light beige fabric, cut 16 squares 1½″ × 1½″ (B) and 2 squares 2⅞″ × 2⅞″ (C).

3. From pink fabric, cut 2 squares 2⅞″ × 2⅞″ (C).

4. Refer to Quick-Pieced Square-On-Point Units (page 14, Air Castle, Step 4) to make 4 quick-pieced square-on-point units with 4 of the dark blue A squares and the 16 light beige B squares.

NOTE: If you prefer, use the B-3: Christmas Eve foundation paper piecing pattern C (page 97) instead. Adapt colors and adjust your fabric cutting accordingly.

5. Refer to Quick-Pieced Half-Square Triangle Units (page 14, Air Castle, Step 5) to make 4 quick-pieced HST units with the light beige C squares and the pink C squares.

6. Sew 2 HST units to opposite sides of a square-on-point unit to make the top row. Press. Repeat to make the bottom row.

7. Sew 2 of the square-on-point units to opposite sides of the remaining dark blue A square to make the center row. Press.

8. Sew the 3 rows together. Press.

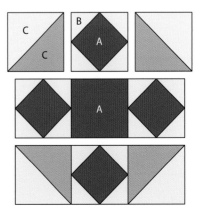

Template patterns A, B, C, and D are on page 95.

1. From light beige fabric, cut
2 squares using template A,
1 rectangle using template B,
12 triangles using template C,
and 4 triangles using template D.

2. From medium blue fabric, cut
8 squares using template A and
4 rectangles using template B.

3. Sew 2 medium blue A squares
to opposite sides of 1 light beige
A square. Press. Repeat to make
a second unit. Sew the units to
opposite sides of the light beige
B rectangle to make the central
square. Press.

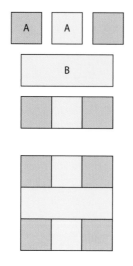

4. Sew 2 light beige C triangles to
opposite sides of a medium blue
A square. Press. Sew 1 light beige
D triangle to an adjacent side. Press.
Repeat to make 4. Sew a medium
blue B rectangle to each unit just
created. Press.

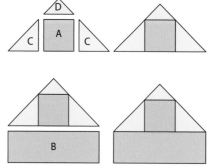

5. Sew 2 light beige C triangles to
opposite ends of the medium blue
B rectangles of a unit created in
the previous step. Press. Repeat to
make 2.

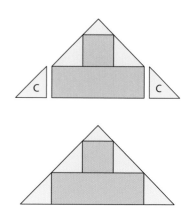

6. Sew the 2 units created in Step 4
to opposite sides of the central
square, as shown. Press.

7. Sew the 2 units created in Step 5
to the remaining sides of the central
square. Press.

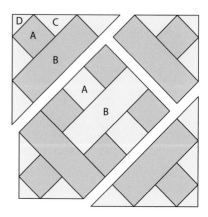

Template patterns A and C are on page 95, and the appliqué placement diagram is on page 96.

1. From light beige fabric, cut 1 square 6½″ × 6½″ (D). Fold the square in half vertically, horizontally, and diagonally both ways, pressing after each fold to mark the appliqué placement lines.

NOTE: You can also cut the square larger and trim to correct size after sewing the appliqué pieces in place, if desired.

2. From pink fabric, cut 8 hearts using template A, adding the required seam allowance for your preferred appliqué method.

🌿 *Tip*

If you are going to zigzag stitch around the appliqué edges, you don't need to add seam allowances; if you prefer to turn under the edges, add a scant ¼″ seam allowance all around and hand or machine straight stitch the appliqué pieces in place.

3. From medium green fabric, cut 20 of leaf template C, adding the required seam allowance for your preferred appliqué method. Cut a bias strip ³⁄₁₆″ × 15″ from medium green fabric for the vine.

NOTE: If you prefer, cut a circle using the appliqué placement diagram as a template, or you can embroider the B vine.

4. Following the appliqué placement diagram (page 96), stitch the appliqué pieces to the light beige D square in this order: 4 center A hearts, B vine, C leaves, 4 corner A hearts.

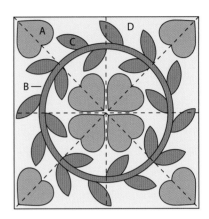

Foundation patterns A, B, and C are on pages 95 and 97.

1. Make 4 of foundation paper piecing pattern A using light beige and red fabrics.

2. Make 4 of foundation paper piecing pattern B using light beige, red, and gold fabrics.

3. Make 1 of foundation paper piecing pattern C using red and gold fabrics.

4. Sew 2 A foundations to opposite sides of a B foundation to make the top row. Press. Repeat to make the bottom row.

5. Sew 2 B foundations to opposite sides of the C foundation to make the center row. Press.

6. Sew the 3 rows together. Press.

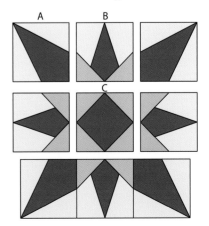

1. From light beige fabric, cut
2 squares 2⅞″ × 2⅞″ (A), cut 1 strip
1½″ × 12″ (B), and cut 1 square
2½″ × 2½″ (C).

2. From medium blue fabric, cut
2 squares 2⅞″ × 2⅞″ (A) and cut
1 strip 1½″ × 12″ (B).

3. Refer to Quick-Pieced Half-Square Triangle Units (page 14, Air Castle, Step 5) to make 4 quick-pieced HST units with the light beige A squares and the medium blue A squares.

4. Sew the light beige B strip and the medium blue B strip together lengthwise. Press toward the medium blue fabric. Use a rotary cutter to crosscut the strip set into 4 strips 2½″ wide.

5. Sew 2 HST units to opposite sides of a unit created in Step 4 to make the top row. Press. Repeat to make the bottom row.

6. Sew 2 units created in Step 4 to the opposite sides of light beige C square to make the center row. Press.

7. Sew the 3 rows together. Press.

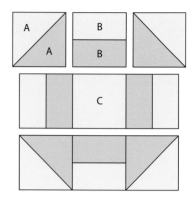

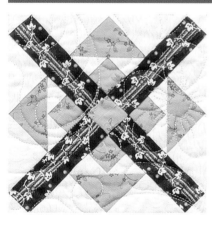

Foundation patterns A, B, and C are on page 96.

1. Make 2 of foundation paper piecing pattern A using light beige and gold fabrics.

2. Make 2 of foundation paper piecing pattern B using light beige, gold, and red fabrics.

3. Make 1 of foundation paper piecing pattern C using light beige, gold, and red fabrics.

4. Sew each A foundation to a B foundation. Press.

5. Sew the A/B foundations pairs to opposite sides of the C foundation. Press.

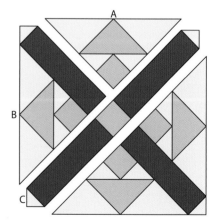

Cock's Comb ❀ BLOCK B-6

Foundation patterns A and B are on page 97.

1. Make 2 of foundation paper piecing pattern A using dark blue and light beige fabrics.

2. Make 2 of foundation paper piecing pattern B using dark blue and light beige fabrics.

3. Sew a Foundation A to a Foundation B to make a block half. Press. Repeat to make a second block half.

4. Sew the halves together. Press.

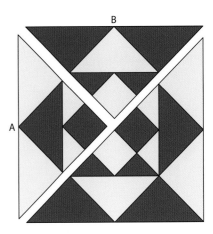

Confluence ❀ BLOCK B-7

Foundation patterns A and B are on page 97.

1. Make 2 of foundation paper piecing pattern A using light beige and pink fabrics.

2. Make 2 of foundation paper piecing pattern B using light beige and medium green fabrics.

3. Sew each A foundation to a B foundation. Press.

4. Sew the 2 rows together. Press.

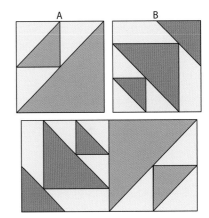

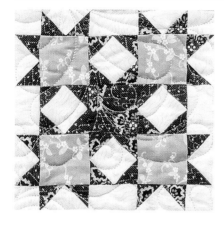

Optional foundation pattern G is on page 97.

1. From medium blue fabric, cut 4 squares 2″ × 2″ (A).

2. From dark blue fabric, cut 1 square 2″ × 2″ (A), 16 squares 1¼″ × 1¼″ (B), and 8 squares 1⅝″ × 1⅝″ (D).

3. From light beige fabric, cut 4 squares 2″ × 2″ (A), 2 squares 2¾″ × 2¾″ (C), 4 rectangles 1¼″ × 2″ (E), and 4 squares 1¼″ × 1¼″ (F).

4. Refer to Quick-Pieced Square-On-Point Units (page 14, Air Castle, Step 4) to make 4 quick-pieced square-on-point units with 4 light beige A squares and 16 dark blue B squares.

NOTE: If you prefer, use the B-8: Corner Star foundation paper piecing pattern G (page 97) instead. Adjust your fabric cutting accordingly.

5. *Quick-Pieced Flying Geese Units:* Make 8 quick-pieced Flying Geese units.

a. Draw a diagonal line from corner to corner on the wrong side of 4 dark blue D squares.

b. Place 2 dark blue D squares on top of a light beige C square, right sides facing, corners overlapping, and drawn lines aligned.

c. Sew a scant ¼″ on both sides of the drawn lines. Cut apart on the drawn lines. Press toward the darker fabric.

d. Place a dark blue D square on one of the units created in Step c, right sides facing, with the drawn line at a right angle to the previous seam. Sew a scant ¼″ on both sides of the drawn line. Cut on the drawn line. Press toward the dark blue fabric to make 2 Flying Geese units.

e. Repeat Step d with the remaining unit created in Step c and a dark blue D square to make 2 more Flying Geese units.

f. Repeat Steps b–e with 4 dark blue D squares and the remaining light beige C square to make 4 more Flying Geese units for a total of 8 Flying Geese units.

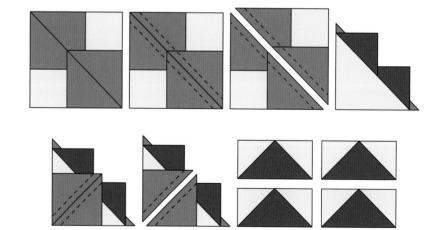

6. Sew 2 medium blue A squares to opposite sides of 1 square-on-point unit. Press toward the medium blue A square. Repeat to make an identical row. Sew 2 square-on-point units to opposite sides of the dark blue A square. Press toward the dark blue A square. Sew the 3 rows together to complete the central pieced square. Press.

7. Sew 2 Flying Geese units to opposite sides of each light beige E rectangle. Press.

8. Sew 2 of the units created in Step 7 to opposite sides of the central pieced square to create the center row. Press.

9. Sew 2 light beige F squares to the opposite ends of the remaining units. Press.

10. Sew the rows created in the previous step to the top and bottom of the center row. Press.

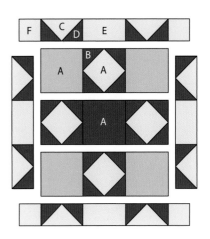

Oak Leaves ❧ BLOCK B-9

Template patterns A, B, and C and the appliqué placement diagram are on page 98.

1. From light beige fabric, cut 1 square 6½″ × 6½″ (D). Fold the square in half vertically, horizontally, and diagonally both ways, pressing after each fold to mark the appliqué placement lines.

NOTE: You can also cut the square larger and trim to size after sewing the appliqué pieces in place, if desired.

2. From medium green fabric, cut 4 large leaves using template A, adding the required seam allowance for your preferred appliqué method.

3. From medium green fabric, cut 4 small leaves using template B, adding the required seam allowance for your preferred appliqué method.

4. From gold fabric, cut 1 of the center using template C, adding the required seam allowance for your preferred appliqué method.

5. Following the appliqué placement diagram (page 98), stitch the appliqué pieces to the light beige D square in this order: A large leaves, B small leaves, C center.

Template pattern E is on page 98.

1. From light beige fabric:

• Cut 4 squares 1⅞″ × 1⅞″ (A).

• Cut 8 squares 1½″ × 1½″ (B).

• Cut 1 square 2½″ × 2½″ (C).

• Cut 1 square 3¼″ × 3¼″. Cut the square in half diagonally twice to make 4 D triangles.

2. From red fabric, cut 4 squares 1⅞″ × 1⅞″ (A) and 4 squares 1½″ × 1½″ (F).

3. From medium blue fabric, cut 4 from template E. Flip the template and cut 4 E Reverse.

4. Refer to Quick-Pieced Half-Square Triangle Units (page 14, Air Castle, Step 5) to make 8 quick-pieced HST units with 4 red A squares and 4 light beige A squares.

5. Sew each HST unit to a light beige B square. Sew together to make 1 block corner, as shown. Repeat to make a total of 4 block corners.

6. Refer to Quick-Pieced Square-On-Point Units (page 14, Air Castle, Step 4) to make 1 quick-pieced square-on-point unit with the light beige C square and the 4 red F squares.

NOTE: If you prefer, use the B-3: Christmas Eve foundation paper piecing pattern C (page 97) instead. Adapt colors and adjust your fabric cutting accordingly.

7. Sewing only from point to point and not into the seam allowances, and sewing only the shorter of the 2 parallel sides, sew each medium blue E to an E Reverse. Press. Using Y-seam construction, attach 1 light beige D triangle to each E/E Reverse pair. Press.

8. Following the assembly diagram for correct alignment, sew 2 block corners to a unit created in Step 7 to create the top row. Press. Repeat to create the bottom row.

9. Sew 2 units created in Step 7 to opposite sides of the square-on-point unit to create the center row. Press.

10. Sew the 3 rows together. Press.

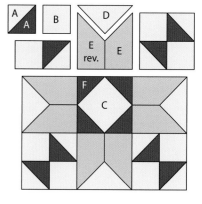

1. From light beige fabric, cut 5 squares 2½″ × 2½″ (A) and 8 squares 1⅞″ × 1⅞″ (D).

2. From medium green fabric, cut 8 squares 1½″ × 1½″ (B) and 2 squares 3¼″ × 3¼″ (C).

3. Draw a diagonal line from corner to corner on the back of each B square. Matching one corner and aligning adjacent sides, place a medium green B square on a light beige A square. Sew on the drawn line. Trim fabric ¼″ away from the sewn line. Press the seam toward the medium green fabric.

Repeat with a second medium green B square in the opposite corner to make a block corner. Repeat to make a total of 4 block corners.

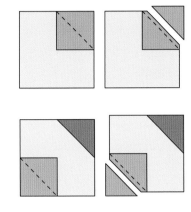

4. Refer to Quick-Pieced Flying Geese Units (page 26, Corner Star, Step 5) to make 8 quick-pieced Flying Geese units with the light beige D squares and the medium green C squares.

5. Sew the Flying Geese units into 4 pairs.

6. Sew 2 block corners to opposite sides of a Flying Geese pair to make the top row. Press. Repeat to make the bottom row.

7. Sew 2 Flying Geese units to opposite sides of the remaining light beige A square to make the center row. Press.

8. Sew the 3 rows together. Press.

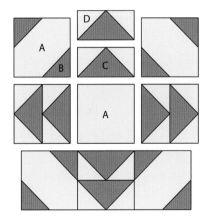

Template pattern D is on page 98.

1. From light beige fabric:

• Cut 2 squares 2⅞″ × 2⅞″ (A).

• Cut 8 squares 1⅞″ × 1⅞″. Cut each square in half diagonally once to make 16 triangles (B).

• Cut 8 squares using template D.

• Cut 4 squares 1½″ × 1½″ (E).

2. From gold fabric, cut 2 squares 2⅞″ × 2⅞″ (A), 1 square 2½″ × 2½″ (C), and 8 squares using template D.

3. Sew each light beige D square to a gold D square. Press. Sew the units together in pairs to make 4 Four-Patch units. Press.

4. Sew 2 light beige B triangles to opposite sides of 1 Four-Patch. Press. Sew 2 light beige B triangles to the other 2 sides. Press. Repeat for each Four-Patch.

5. Refer to Quick-Pieced Half-Square Triangle Units (page 14, Air Castle, Step 5) to make 4 quick-pieced HST units with the gold A squares and the light beige A squares.

6. Refer to Quick-Pieced Square-On-Point Units (page 14, Air Castle, Step 4) to make 1 quick-pieced square-on-point unit with the gold C square and the light beige E squares.

NOTE: If you prefer, use the B-3: Christmas Eve foundation paper piecing pattern C (page 97) instead. Adapt colors and adjust your fabric cutting accordingly.

7. Sew 2 HST units to opposite sides of a unit created in Step 4 to make the top row. Press. Repeat to make the bottom row.

8. Sew the remaining 2 units created in Step 4 to opposite sides of the square-on-point unit to make the center row. Press.

9. Sew the 3 rows together. Press.

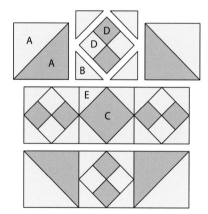

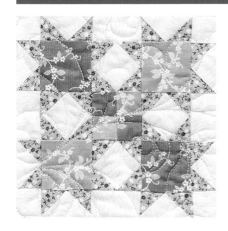

1. From pink fabric, cut 16 squares 1¼″ × 1¼″ (B) and 8 squares 1⅝″ × 1⅝″ (D).

2. From medium blue fabric, cut 2 squares 2″ × 2″ (A) and 2 squares 1¼″ × 1¼″ (F).

3. From medium green fabric, cut 2 squares 2″ × 2″ (A) and 2 squares 1¼″ × 1¼″ (F).

4. From light beige fabric, cut 4 squares 2″ × 2″ (A), 2 squares 2¾″ × 2¾″ (C), 4 rectangles 1¼″ × 2″ (D), and 4 squares 1¼″ × 1¼″ (F).

5. Refer to Quick-Pieced Square-On-Point Units (page 14, Air Castle, Step 4) to make 4 quick-pieced square-on-point units with the light beige A squares and the pink B squares.

NOTE: If you prefer, use the B-8: Corner Star foundation paper piecing pattern G (page 97) instead. Adapt colors and adjust your fabric cutting accordingly.

6. Refer to Quick-Pieced Flying Geese Units (page 26, Corner Star, Step 5) to make 8 quick-pieced Flying Geese units with the pink D squares and the light beige C squares.

7. Sew 1 medium blue F square to a medium green F square. Press toward the medium green fabric. Repeat. Sew the 2 F/F pairs together to make the central Four-Patch. Press.

8. Sew 1 medium blue A square and 1 medium green A square to opposite sides of 1 square-on-point unit. Press toward the A squares.

Repeat to make an identical row. Sew 2 square-on-point units to opposite sides of the central Four-Patch. Press toward the Four-Patch. Sew the 3 rows together to complete the central pieced square. Press.

9. Sew 2 Flying Geese units to opposite sides of each light beige E rectangle. Press.

10. Sew 2 of the units created in Step 9 to opposite sides of the central pieced square to create the center row. Press.

11. Sew 2 light beige F squares to the opposite ends of the remaining units. Press.

12. Sew the rows created in the previous step to the top and bottom of the center row. Press.

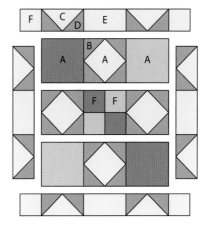

1. From light beige fabric, cut 4 squares 1⅝″ × 1⅝″ (A), 12 squares 1¼″ × 1¼″ (B), 2 squares 2¾″ × 2¾″ (C), and 4 squares 2″ × 2″ (D).

2. From medium blue fabric, cut 4 squares 1⅝″ × 1⅝″ (A) and 1 square 2″ × 2″ (D).

3. From red fabric, cut 8 squares 1⅝″ × 1⅝″ (A) and 4 rectangles 1¼″ × 2″ (E).

4. Refer to Quick-Pieced Half-Square Triangle Units (page 14, Air Castle, Step 5) to make 8 quick-pieced HST units with 4 red A squares and 4 light beige A squares.

5. Refer to Quick-Pieced Flying Geese Units (page 26, Corner Star, Step 5) to make 4 quick-pieced Flying Geese units with the 4 medium blue B squares and a light beige C square. Make 4 quick-pieced Flying Geese units with 4 red B squares and a light beige C square.

6. Sew 2 medium blue/light beige Flying Geese units to opposite sides of the medium blue D square. Press.

7. Sew 2 light beige B squares to opposite ends of each remaining medium blue/light beige and red/light beige Flying Geese unit. Press.

8. Sew 2 medium blue/light beige units created in Step 7 to opposite sides of the medium blue D unit to create the central star. Press.

9. Sew 2 red/light beige triangle-squares to opposite ends of the red E rectangles. Press. Sew each of these units to a red/light beige Flying Geese unit created in Step 7. Press.

10. Sew 2 of the units created in Step 9 to opposite sides of the central star to create the center row. Press.

11. Sew 2 light beige D squares to opposite ends of a unit created in Step 9 to create the top row. Press. Repeat to create the bottom row.

12. Sew the 3 rows together. Press.

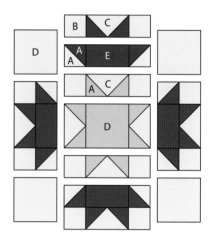

1. From light beige fabric:

• Cut 1 square 2½″ × 2½″ (A).

• Cut 2 squares 2⅞″ × 2⅞″. Cut each square in half diagonally once to make 4 triangles (D).

2. From light green fabric, cut 2 squares 3¼″ × 3¼″ (B) and 4 squares 1½″ × 1½″ (C).

3. From dark blue fabric:

• Cut 2 squares 3¼″ × 3¼″ (B).

• Cut 4 squares 1⅞″ × 1⅞″. Cut each square in half diagonally once to make 8 triangles (E).

4. Sew 2 dark blue E triangles to adjacent sides of each light green C square. Press. Sew 1 light beige D triangle to each unit to make 4 block corners. Press.

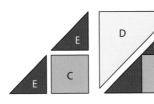

5. Refer to Quick-Pieced Quarter-Square Triangle Units (page 16, Blocks and Stars, Step 5) to make 4 quick-pieced QST units with the light green B squares and the dark blue B squares.

6. Sew 2 corner units to opposite sides of a QST unit to make the top row. Press. Repeat for the bottom row.

7. Sew the remaining 2 QST units to opposite sides of the light beige A square to make the center row. Press.

8. Sew the 3 rows together. Press.

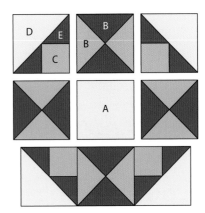

Template pattern C is on page 99.

1. From light beige fabric, cut 4 squares 2½″ × 2½″ (A), 1 square 3¼″ × 3¼″ (B), and 5 squares using template C.

2. From gold fabric, cut 2 squares 3¼″ × 3¼″ (B) and 4 squares using template C.

3. From dark blue fabric, cut 1 square 3¼″ × 3¼″ (B).

4. Sew 2 light beige C squares to opposite sides of 1 gold C square to make the top row of the central Nine-Patch unit. Press toward the gold fabric. Repeat to make the bottom row. Sew 2 gold C squares to opposite sides of the remaining light beige C square to make the center row. Press. Sew the 3 rows together to make the central Nine-Patch unit.

5. *Quick-Pieced Quarter-Square Triangle Variation Units:* Make 4 quick-pieced quarter-square triangle variations:

a. Draw a diagonal line from corner to corner on the wrong side of each gold B square.

b. Pair a gold B square with a dark blue B square, right sides facing. Sew ¼″ on both sides of the drawn line.

c. Cut on the solid line to make 2 HST units. Press toward the dark blue fabric.

d. Repeat Steps b and c with the remaining gold B square and the light beige B square to make 2 additional HST units.

e. On the wrong side of the gold/light beige HST units, draw a diagonal line from a gold corner to a light beige corner.

f. Place the marked gold/light beige HST unit and a gold/dark blue HST unit together with right sides facing and the gold triangles opposite each other. Align edges, abut opposing seams, and pin. Sew ¼″ on both sides of the drawn line.

g. Cut on the drawn line to yield 2 QST variation units. Press. Repeat with the remaining HST units to make 2 more QST variation units.

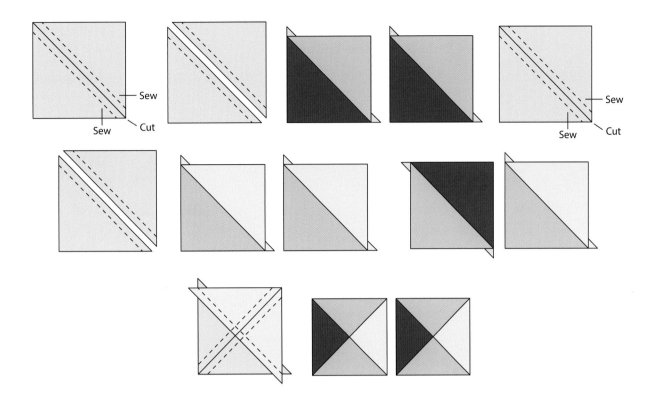

6. Noting correct color placement, sew 2 light beige A squares to opposite sides of a QST variation unit to make the top row. Press. Repeat to make the bottom row.

7. Noting correct color placement, sew 2 QST variation units to opposite sides of the Nine-Patch unit to make the center row. Press.

8. Sew the 3 rows together. Press.

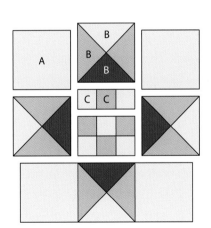

Double Pinwheel ✿ BLOCK C-7

Foundation patterns A and B are on page 98.

1. Make 4 of foundation paper piecing pattern A using medium green, medium blue, and light beige fabrics.

2. Make 4 of foundation paper piecing pattern B using medium green, medium blue, and light beige fabrics.

3. Sew an A triangle to a B triangle along the longest side to make a block quarter. Press. Repeat to make 4.

4. Sew the block quarters together in pairs to make 2 rows. Press.

5. Sew the rows together. Press.

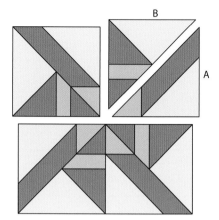

Double Quartet ✿ BLOCK C-8

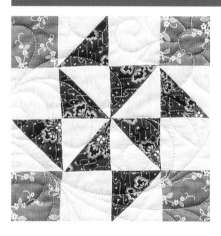

1. From light beige fabric, cut 4 squares 2⅜″ × 2⅜″ (A) and 4 squares 2″ × 2″ (B).

2. From red fabric, cut 4 squares 2⅜″ × 2⅜″ (A).

3. From medium green fabric, cut 4 squares 2″ × 2″ (B).

4. Refer to Quick-Pieced Half-Square Triangle Units (page 14, Air Castle, Step 5) to make 8 quick-pieced HST units with the red A squares and the light beige A squares.

5. Noting correct color placement, sew 2 HST units together. Press. Repeat to make a second HST unit pair. Sew the 2 pairs together to make the central pinwheel. Press.

6. Sew a light beige B square to each remaining HST unit, as shown. Press.

7. Sew 2 of the units created in the previous step to opposite sides of the central pinwheel to make the center row. Press.

8. Sew 2 medium green B squares to opposite ends of another unit created in Step 6 to make the top row. Press. Repeat to make the bottom row.

9. Sew the 3 rows together. Press.

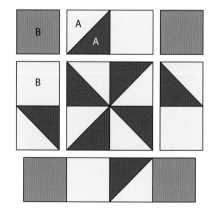

Double Z ✾ BLOCK C-9

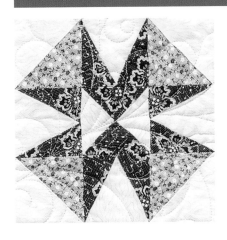

Foundation patterns A and B are on page 99.

1. Make 2 of foundation paper piecing pattern A using pink, dark blue, and light beige fabrics.

2. Make 2 of foundation paper piecing pattern B using dark blue and light beige fabrics.

3. Sew the 2 B foundations together to make the center row. Press.

4. Sew the 2 A foundations to the top and bottom of the center row. Press.

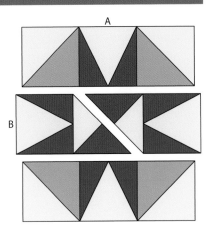

Duck Tracks ✾ BLOCK C-10

Template pattern D is on page 99.

1. From light beige fabric:

• Cut 4 squares 2⅜″ × 2⅜″ (A). Cut 2 of the A squares in half diagonally once to make 4 triangles (B).

• Cut 4 squares 2″ × 2″ (C).

2. From dark blue fabric, cut 2 squares 2⅜″ × 2⅜″ (A).

3. Using template D, cut 2 from medium blue fabric and 2 from medium green fabric.

4. Sew 1 light beige B triangle to each D. Press.

5. Refer to Quick-Pieced Half-Square Triangle Units (page 14, Air Castle, Step 5) to make 4 quick-pieced HST units with the dark blue A squares and the light beige A squares.

6. Sew each HST unit to a light beige C square. Press.

7. Sew each unit created in Step 6 to a unit created in Step 4 to make 4 block quarters, as shown. Press.

8. Following the block assembly diagram for correct orientation, sew the block quarters into pairs to make 2 rows. Press.

9. Sew the rows together. Press.

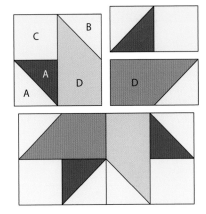

Foundation pattern E is on page 99.

1. From light beige fabric, cut 4 squares 2¼″ × 2¼″ (A), 4 squares 1⅞″ × 1⅞″ (B), and 4 rectangles 1″ × 3¼″ (C).

2. From pink fabric, cut 4 squares 2¼″ × 2¼″ (A).

3. From red fabric, cut 1 square 1″ × 1″ (D).

4. Make 4 of foundation paper piecing pattern E using red and pink fabrics.

5. Refer to Quick-Pieced Half-Square Triangle Units (page 14, Air Castle, Step 5) to make 8 quick-pieced HST units with the pink A squares and the light beige A squares.

6. Following the assembly diagram for correct orientation, sew 1 HST unit to each E foundation. Press.

7. Following the assembly diagram for correct orientation, sew 1 light beige B square to each remaining HST unit. Press.

8. Sew each unit created in Step 6 to a unit created in Step 7 to make 4 block corners. Press.

9. Sew 2 units created in Step 8 to opposite sides of a light beige C rectangle to create the top row. Press. Repeat to create the bottom row.

10. Sew the remaining 2 light beige C rectangles to opposite sides of the red D square to make the center row. Press.

11. Sew the 3 rows together. Press.

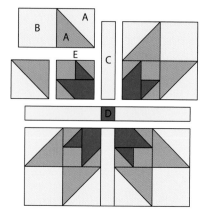

Foundation pattern C is on page 99.

1. From light beige fabric, cut 4 rectangles 1½″ × 3″ (A).

2. From medium green fabric, cut 1 square 1½″ × 1½″ (B).

3. Make 1 of foundation paper piecing pattern C using light beige fabric and medium blue fabrics. Repeat to make 3 additional C foundations, 1 with light beige and light green fabrics, 1 with light beige and pink fabrics, and 1 with light beige and gold fabrics.

4. Sew 2 C foundations to opposite sides of 1 light beige A rectangle to make the top row. Press. Repeat to make the bottom row.

5. Sew the remaining 2 light beige A rectangles to opposite sides of the medium green B square to make the center row. Press.

6. Sew the 3 rows together. Press.

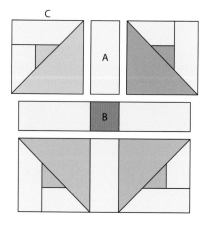

1. From light beige fabric, cut 2 strips 1″ × 14″ (A), 2 squares 1″ × 1″ (B), and 2 squares 3⅛″ × 3⅛″ (C).

2. From dark blue fabric, cut 1 strip 1″ × 14″ (A), 4 squares 1″ × 1″ (B), and 2 squares 3⅛″ × 3⅛″ (C).

3. Sew the 2 light beige A strips to opposite sides of the dark blue A strip. Press toward the dark blue fabric. Use a rotary to crosscut the strip set to make 4 strips 2″ × 2¾″. Crosscut once more to make 1 strip 1″ × 2″.

4. Sew 2 dark blue B squares to opposite sides of each light beige B square. Press toward the dark blue fabric. Sew each of these strips to opposite sides of the 1″ × 2″ strip from Step 3 to make the center Nine-Patch unit. Press.

5. Refer to Quick-Pieced Half-Square Triangle Units (page 14, Air Castle, Step 5) to make 4 quick-pieced HST units with the light beige C squares and dark blue C squares.

6. Following the assembly diagram for correct alignment, sew 2 HST units to opposite sides of an A/A/A strip to make the top row. Press. Repeat to make the bottom row.

7. Sew the remaining A/A/A strips to opposite sides of the center Nine-Patch unit to make the center row. Press.

8. Sew the 3 rows together. Press.

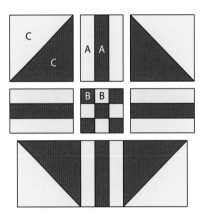

Flying Birds ❧ BLOCK D-4

Foundation pattern B is on page 99.

1. From light beige fabric, cut 3 squares 2½″ × 2½″ (A).

2. Make 6 of foundation paper piecing pattern B using light beige and medium blue fabrics.

3. Following the assembly diagram for correct orientation, sew 2 B foundations and 1 light beige A square to make the top row. Press. Repeat with 2 more B foundations and 1 light beige A square to make the center row. Press. Repeat with the remaining 2 B foundations and 1 light beige A square to make the bottom row. Press.

4. Sew the 3 rows together. Press.

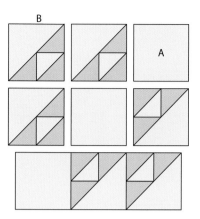

Forever Friends ❧ BLOCK D-5

Template patterns C and D are on page 99.

1. From light beige fabric, cut 2 squares 2⅞″ × 2⅞″ (A) and 4 squares 2½″ × 2½″ (B).

2. From medium green fabric, cut 2 squares 2⅞″ × 2⅞″ (A). Cut 4 squares using template C. Cut 4 triangles using template D.

3. From gold fabric, cut 1 square using template C. Cut 4 triangles using template D.

4. Make the central star.

a. Pair a gold D triangle with a medium green D triangle. Sew along the longest edge. Press toward the medium green fabric. Repeat to make a total of 4 medium green/gold half-square triangle units.

b. Sew 2 medium green C squares to opposite sides of 1 gold/medium green HST unit to make the top row. Press toward the C squares. Repeat to make the bottom row.

c. Sew 2 gold/medium green HST units to opposite sides of the gold C square to make the center row. Press toward the C square.

d. Sew the 3 rows together. Press.

5. Refer to Quick-Pieced Half-Square Triangle Units (page 14, Air Castle, Step 5) to make 4 quick-pieced HST units with the medium green A squares and the light beige A squares.

6. Sew 2 light beige B squares to opposite sides of a light beige/medium green HST unit to make the top row. Press toward the B squares. Repeat to make the bottom row.

7. Following the assembly diagram for correct orientation, sew 2 light beige/medium green HST units to opposite sides of the central star to make the center row. Press.

8. Sew the 3 rows together. Press.

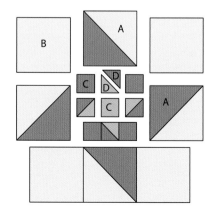

Fort Bridger ✺ BLOCK D-6

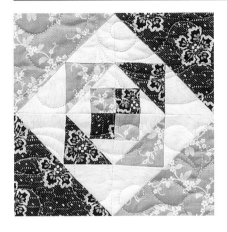

Foundation pattern A is on page 100.

1. Make 2 of foundation paper piecing pattern A using dark blue and light beige fabrics.

2. Make 2 of foundation paper piecing pattern A using medium blue and light beige fabrics.

3. Sew each dark blue/light beige A foundation to a medium blue/light beige A foundation as shown in the assembly diagram to make 2 rows. Press.

4. Sew the rows together. Press.

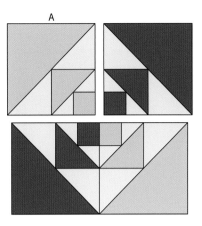

Four-Patch Star ✺ BLOCK D-7

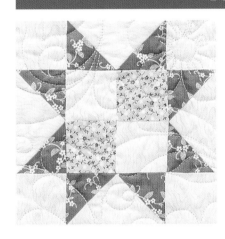

1. From light beige fabric, cut 1 square 4¼″ × 4¼″ (A) and 6 squares 2″ × 2″ (C).

2. From light green fabric, cut 2 squares 2″ × 2″ (C).

3. From medium green fabric, cut 4 squares 2⅜″ × 2⅜″ (B).

4. Refer to Quick-Pieced Flying Geese Units (page 26, Corner Star, Step 5) to make 4 quick-pieced Flying Geese units with the medium green B squares and the light beige A square.

5. Sew each light green C square to a light beige C square. Press toward the light green fabric. Sew the 2 units together to make the central Four-Patch unit. Press.

6. Following the assembly diagram for correct orientation, sew 2 Flying Geese units to opposite sides of the Four-Patch unit to make the center row. Press.

7. Sew 2 light beige C squares to opposite ends of a Flying Geese unit to make the top row. Press. Repeat to make the bottom row.

8. Sew the 3 rows together. Press.

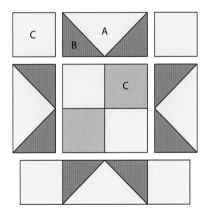

Template pattern A is on page 99.

1. From gold fabric:

• Cut 4 squares using template A.

• Cut 3 squares 2¾″ × 2¾″. Cut each in half diagonally twice to make 12 triangles (B).

2. From red fabric:

• Cut 2 squares 2¾″ × 2¾″. Cut each in half diagonally twice to make 8 triangles (B).

• Cut 1 square 2″ × 2″ (C).

3. From light beige fabric:

• Cut 2 squares 2¾″ × 2¾″. Cut each in half diagonally twice to make 8 B triangles.

• Cut 4 squares 2″ × 2″ (C).

• Cut 2 squares 2⅜″ × 2⅜″. Cut each in half diagonally once to make 4 D triangles.

4. Sew 2 gold B triangles to opposite sides of the red C square. Press. Sew the other 2 gold B triangles to the remaining sides. Press. Sew 2 light beige D triangles to opposite sides of the unit. Press. Sew on the remaining light beige D triangles to complete the block center. Press.

5. Sew 2 red B triangles to adjacent sides of a gold A square. Press toward the gold fabric. Repeat to make 4.

6. Sew each light beige B triangle to a gold B triangle, noting color placement to make 4 B/B units and 4 mirror-image B/B units. Press toward the gold fabric.

7. Sew 1 B/B unit and 1 B/B mirror-image unit to each A/B/B unit. Press. Make 4.

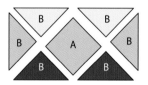

8. Sew 2 light beige C squares to opposite ends of each unit created in Step 7 to create the top row. Press. Repeat to make the bottom row.

9. Sew 2 of the units created in Step 7 to opposite sides of the block center to make the center row. Press.

10. Sew the 3 rows together. Press.

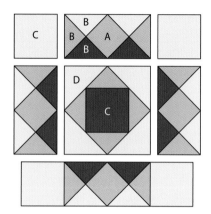

Friendship Chain ❀ BLOCK D-9

Foundation patterns A and B are on page 100.

1. Make 2 of foundation paper piecing pattern A using medium blue, medium green, and light beige fabrics.

2. Make 2 of foundation paper piecing pattern B using medium blue, medium green, and light beige fabrics.

3. Following the assembly diagram for correct alignment, sew an A foundation to a B foundation to make 1 row. Press. Repeat to make a second row.

4. Sew the rows together as shown. Press.

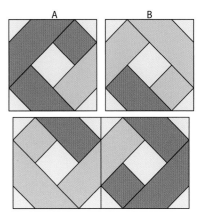

Friendship Quilt ❀ BLOCK D-10

Foundation patterns B and C are on page 100.

1. From light beige fabric, cut 2 squares 2⅜″ × 2⅜″ (A).

2. From dark blue fabric, cut 2 squares 2⅜″ × 2⅜″ (A).

3. Refer to Quick-Pieced Half-Square Triangle Units (page 14, Air Castle, Step 5) to make 4 quick-pieced HST units with the dark blue A squares and the light beige A squares.

4. Make 1 of foundation paper piecing pattern B using dark blue and gold fabrics.

5. Make 4 of foundation paper piecing pattern C using dark blue, gold, and light beige fabrics.

6. Sew 2 C foundations to opposite sides of the B foundation to make the center row. Press.

7. Noting the assembly diagram for correct alignment, sew 2 HST units to opposite sides of a C foundation to make the top row. Press. Repeat to make the bottom row.

8. Sew the 3 rows together. Press.

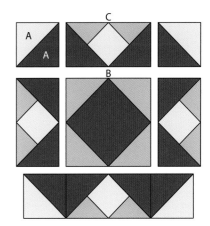

1. From light beige fabric, cut 2 squares 2⅞″ × 2⅞″ (A) and 1 strip 1½″ × 12″ (B).

2. From gold fabric, cut 2 squares 2⅞″ × 2⅞″ (A).

3. From medium green fabric, cut 1 strip 1½″ × 12″ (B) and 1 square 2½″ × 2½″ (C).

4. Refer to Quick-Pieced Half-Square Triangle Units (page 14, Air Castle, Step 5) to make 4 quick-pieced HST units with the gold and light beige A squares.

5. Sew the light beige B strip to the medium green B strip together lengthwise. Press toward the medium green fabric. Use a rotary cutter to crosscut the strip set into 4 strips 2½″ wide.

6. Following the assembly diagram for correct orientation, sew 2 HST units to opposite sides of a B/B strip to make the top row. Press. Repeat to make the bottom row.

7. Following the assembly diagram for correct orientation, sew the 2 remaining B/B strips to opposite sides of the medium green C square to make the center row. Press.

8. Sew the 3 rows together. Press.

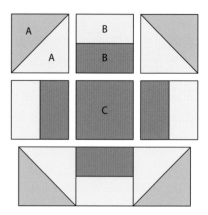

Foundation patterns A and B are on page 100.

1. Make 4 of foundation paper piecing pattern A using medium blue and light beige fabrics.

2. Make 4 of foundation paper piecing pattern B using medium blue and light beige fabrics.

3. Pair each A triangle with a B triangle and sew along the longest edge to make 4 block quarters. Press.

4. Following the assembly diagram for correct orientation, sew the block quarters into pairs to make 2 rows. Press.

5. Sew the rows together. Press.

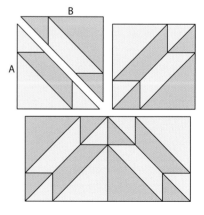

1. From red fabric, cut 1 square 2½″ × 2½″ (A) and 2 squares 3¼″ × 3¼″ (B).

2. From light beige fabric, cut 1 square 3¼″ × 3¼″ (B) and 1 strip 1½″ × 14″ (C).

3. From medium green fabric, cut 1 square 3¼″ × 3¼″ (B) and 1 strip 1½″ × 14″ (C).

4. Sew the light beige C strip to the medium green C strip lengthwise. Press toward the medium green fabric. Use a rotary cutter to crosscut the strip set into 4 strips 1½″ wide. Sew the strips together in pairs to make 4 Four-Patch units.

5. Refer to Quick-Pieced Quarter-Square Triangle Variation Units (pages 34 and 35, Dolley Madison's Star, Step 5) to make 4 quick-pieced QST variation units with the medium green, red, and light beige B squares.

6. Sew 2 Four-Patch units to opposite sides of a QST variation unit to make the top row. Press. Repeat to make the bottom row.

7. Following the assembly diagram for correct orientation, sew 2 QST variation units to opposite sides of the red A square to make the center row. Press.

8. Sew the 3 rows together. Press.

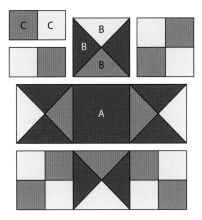

Foundation patterns A and B are on page 101.

1. Make 4 of foundation paper piecing pattern A using dark blue and gold fabrics.

2. Make 4 of foundation paper piecing pattern B using dark blue, gold, and light beige fabrics.

3. Pair each A triangle with a B triangle and sew along the longest edge to make 4 block quarters. Press.

4. Sew the block quarters into pairs to make 2 rows. Press.

5. Sew the rows together. Press.

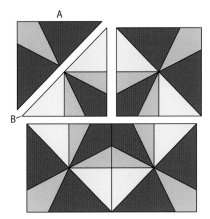

1. From light green fabric, cut 2 squares 2⅞″ × 2⅞″ (A) and 1 square 2½″ × 2½″ (C).

2. From light beige fabric, cut 1 strip 1½″ × 12″ (B).

3. From pink fabric, cut 2 squares 2⅞″ × 2⅞″ (A) and 1 strip 1½″ × 12″ (B).

4. Refer to Quick-Pieced Half-Square Triangle Units (page 14, Air Castle, Step 5) to make 4 quick-pieced HST units with the light green and pink A squares.

5. Sew the light beige B strip and pink B strip together lengthwise. Press toward the pink fabric. Use a rotary cutter to crosscut the strip set into 4 strips 2½″ wide.

6. Sew 2 HST units to opposite sides of a unit created in Step 5 to make the top row. Press. Repeat to make the bottom row.

7. Sew 2 units created in Step 5 to the opposite sides of light green C square to make the center row. Press.

8. Sew the 3 rows together. Press.

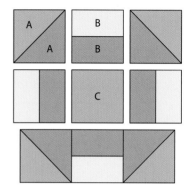

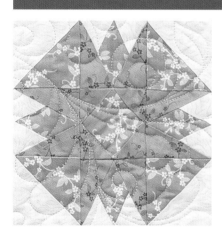

Foundation pattern D is on page 101.

1. From medium blue fabric, cut 1 square 2½″ × 2½″ (A) and 2 squares 2⅞″ × 2⅞″ (C).

2. From gold fabric, cut 4 squares 1½″ × 1½″ (B)

3. From light beige fabric, cut 2 squares 2⅞″ × 2⅞″ (C).

4. Refer to Quick-Pieced Square-On-Point Units (page 14, Air Castle, Step 4) to make 1 quick-pieced square-on-point unit with 1 medium blue A square and 4 gold B squares.

NOTE: If you prefer, use the B-3: Christmas Eve foundation paper piecing pattern C (page 97) instead. Adapt colors and adjust your fabric cutting accordingly.

5. Refer to Quick-Pieced Half-Square Triangle Units (page 14, Air Castle, Step 5) to make 4 quick-pieced HST units with the light beige C squares and the medium blue C squares.

6. Make 4 of foundation paper piecing pattern D using the light beige, gold, and medium blue fabrics.

7. Sew 2 HST units to opposite sides of a D foundation to make the top row. Press. Repeat to make the bottom row.

8. Sew 2 D foundation units to opposite sides of the square-on-point unit to make the center row. Press.

9. Sew the 3 rows together. Press.

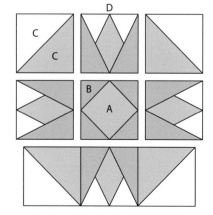

Template pattern A is on page 101.

1. From medium green fabric, cut 8 rhombuses using template A.

2. From dark blue fabric, cut 8 rhombuses using template A and cut 2 squares 1¾″ × 1¾″ (C).

3. From light beige fabric,

• Cut 2 squares 3″ × 3″. Cut each square in half diagonally twice to make 8 triangles (B).

• Cut 6 squares 1¾″ × 1¾″ (C).

4. Sew each dark blue C square to a light beige C square. Press toward the dark blue fabric. Sew the 2 C/C pairs together to make the center Four-Patch unit. Press.

5. Sewing only from point to point and not into the seam allowances, sew each medium green A rhombus to a dark blue A rhombus as shown. Press. Make 4 pairs and 4 mirror-image pairs.

6. Using Y-seam construction, sew 1 light beige B triangle to each A/A rhombus pair. Press.

7. Noting correct color alignment and sewing only from point to point, sew 1 light beige C square to 4 identical A/A/B units. Press. Sew each of these units to a mirror-image A/A/B unit. Sew in the direction of the arrows. Press. Make 4 block corners.

8. Sewing only from point to point and not into the seam allowances, sew 2 block corners to opposite sides of the center Four-Patch unit. Press. Using Y-seam construction, sew the remaining block corners to the other sides. Press.

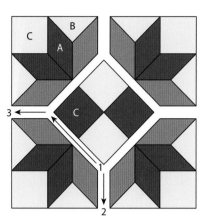

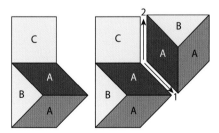

Template patterns A and B are on page 101.

1. From pink fabric, cut 4 kites using template A.

2. From light beige fabric, cut 4 triangles using template B. Flip the template and make 4 B Reverse triangles.

3. From gold fabric, cut 4 rectangles 1½″ × 3″ (C).

4. From medium green fabric, cut 1 square 1½″ × 1½″ (D).

5. Sew 1 light beige B triangle and 1 beige B Reverse triangle to adjacent sides of each pink A kite. Press. Repeat to make 4 block corners.

6. Sew 2 of the units created in Step 5 to opposite sides of a gold C rectangle. Press toward the C rectangle. Repeat to create an identical row.

7. Sew the remaining 2 gold C rectangles to opposite sides of the medium green D square. Press toward the C rectangles.

8. Sew the 3 rows together. Press.

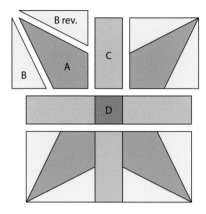

1. From dark blue fabric, cut 4 squares 2½″ × 2½″ (A) and 1 strip 1¼″ × 12″ (C).

2. From light beige fabric, cut 1 square 2½″ × 2½″ (A), 16 squares 1½″ × 1½″ (B), and 2 strips 1⅛″ × 12″ (D).

3. Refer to Quick-Pieced Square-On-Point Units (page 14, Air Castle, Step 4) to make 4 quick-pieced square-on-point units with the dark blue A squares and the light beige B squares.

> **NOTE:** If you prefer, use the B-3: Christmas Eve foundation paper piecing pattern C (page 97) instead. Adapt colors and adjust your fabric cutting accordingly.

4. Sew the 2 light beige C strips to opposite sides of the dark blue D strip. Press toward the dark blue fabric. Use a rotary cutter to crosscut the strip set into 4 strips 2½″ wide.

5. Sew 2 of the square-on-point units to opposite sides of a horizontal strip unit to make the top row. Press. Repeat to make the bottom row.

6. Sew 2 vertical strip units to opposite sides of the light beige A square to make the center row. Press.

7. Sew the 3 rows together. Press.

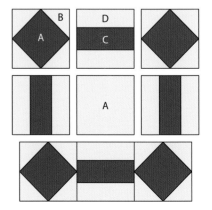

Template patterns A, B, and C are on page 101.

1. From red fabric, cut 4 rhombuses using template A.

2. From light green fabric, cut 4 rhombuses using template A.

3. From light beige fabric, cut 4 triangles using template B and 4 squares using template C.

4. Sewing only from point to point and not into the seam allowances, sew each red A rhombus to a light green A rhombus as shown. Sew in the direction of the arrows. Press. Using Y-seam construction, sew a light beige B triangle to each A/A rhombus pair. Press. Make 4.

5. Sewing from point to point, attach 1 light beige C square to each red A rhombus. Press.

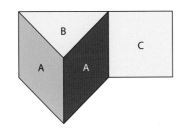

6. Sewing from point to point in the direction of the arrows, sew together 2 A/A/B/C units to make a block half. Press. Repeat to make a second identical unit.

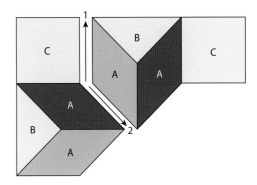

7. Sew the block halves together as shown to complete the block. Press.

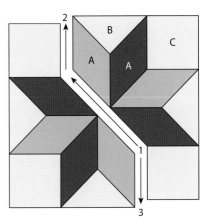

Template pattern A is on page 101, and foundation pattern B is on page 102.

1. From light beige fabric, cut 1 square using template A. Reinforce with freezer paper if desired.

2. Make 4 of foundation paper piecing pattern B using light beige, red, and dark blue fabrics.

3. Following the assembly diagram, sew the paper pieced segments to the light beige A square in numerical order, using the partial seams piecing method:

a. When attaching the first segment, sew only part of the way along the edge, as indicated by the arrow.

b. Sew the second and third segments using a complete seam. Carefully fold the first segment out of the way when attaching the last segment.

c. After attaching the fourth segment, complete the partial seam for the first segment. Press.

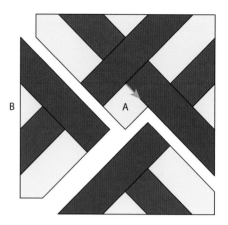

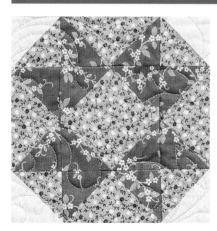

1. From pink fabric, cut 1 square 4¼″ × 4¼″ (B), 1 square 3½″ × 3½″ (C), and 2 squares 2⅜″ × 2⅜″ (D).

2. From medium green fabric, cut 4 squares 2″ × 2″ (A) and 4 squares 2⅜″ × 2⅜″ (D).

3. From light beige fabric, cut 2 squares 2⅜″ × 2⅜″ (D).

4. Refer to Quick-Pieced Flying Geese Units (page 26, Corner Star, Step 5) to make 4 quick-pieced Flying Geese units with the pink B square and the medium green D squares.

5. Refer to Quick-Pieced Square-On-Point Units (page 14, Air Castle, Step 4) to make 1 quick-pieced square-on-point unit with the medium green A squares and the pink C square.

6. Refer to Quick-Pieced Half-Square Triangle Units (page 14, Air Castle, Step 5) to make 4 quick-pieced HST units with the pink D squares and the light beige D squares.

7. Sew 2 HST units to opposite sides of a Flying Geese unit to make the top row. Press. Repeat to make the bottom row.

8. Sew 2 Flying Geese units to opposite sides of the square-on-point unit to make the center row. Press.

9. Sew the 3 rows together. Press.

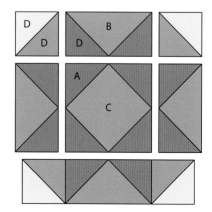

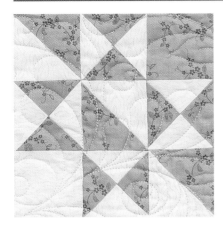

1. From light beige fabric, cut
2 squares 2⅞″ × 2⅞″ (A),
2 squares 3¼″ × 3¼″ (B), and
1 square 2½″ × 2½″ (C).

2. From gold fabric, cut
2 squares 2⅞″ × 2⅞″ (A),
2 squares 3¼″ × 3¼″ (B), and
1 square 2½″ × 2½″ (C).

3. Refer to Quick-Pieced Half-Square Triangle Units (page 14, Air Castle, Step 5) to make 4 quick-pieced HST units with the gold A squares and the light beige A squares.

NOTE: You need only 3 HST units for this block so you will have one unit left over.

4. Refer to Quick-Pieced Quarter-Square Triangle Units (page 16, Blocks and Stars, Step 5) to make 4 quick-pieced QST units with the light beige B squares and the gold B squares.

5. Following the assembly diagram for correct alignment, sew 1 HST unit, 1 QST unit, and the gold C square together to make the top row. Press.

6. Following the assembly diagram for correct alignment, sew 2 QST units to opposite sides of an HST to make the center row. Press.

7. Following the assembly diagram for correct alignment, sew 1 HST unit, 1 QST unit, and the light beige C square together to make the bottom row. Press.

8. Sew the 3 rows together. Press.

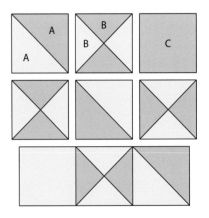

Foundation patterns A, B, and C are on pages 101 and 103.

1. Make 4 of foundation paper piecing pattern A using dark blue and light beige fabrics.

2. Make 4 of foundation paper piecing pattern B using medium green and light beige fabrics.

3. Make 1 of foundation paper piecing pattern C using dark blue and light beige fabrics.

4. Sew 2 A foundations to opposite sides of a B foundation to make the top row. Press. Repeat to make the bottom row.

5. Sew 2 B foundations to opposite sides of the C foundation to make the center row. Press.

6. Sew the 3 rows together. Press.

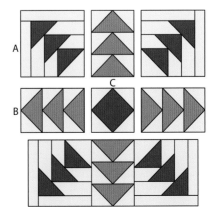

1. From light beige fabric, cut 4 squares 2⅝″ × 2⅝″ (A), 4 squares 1⅞″ × 1⅞″ (B), and 4 rectangles 1″ × 3¼″ (C).

2. From medium blue fabric, cut 4 squares 2⅝″ × 2⅝″ (A), 4 squares 1⅞″ × 1⅞″ (B), and 1 square 1″ × 1″ (D).

3. Refer to Quick-Pieced Quarter-Square Triangle Units (page 16, Blocks and Stars, Step 5) to make 8 quick-pieced QST units with the light beige A squares and the medium blue A squares.

4. Noting correct alignment, sew a QST unit to a light beige B square. Repeat to make 4. Sew a QST unit to a medium blue B square. Repeat to make 4. Press toward the B squares.

5. Following the assembly diagram for correct alignment, sew the units created in Step 4 together to make a block corner. Make 4 block corners.

6. Sew 2 block corners to opposite sides of a light beige C rectangle to make the top row. Repeat to make the bottom row. Press.

7. Sew the 2 remaining light beige C rectangles to opposite sides of the medium blue D square to make the center row. Press.

8. Sew the 3 rows together. Press.

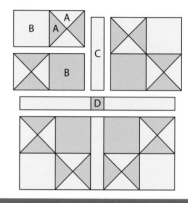

1. From light beige fabric:

- Cut 1 square 2½″ × 2½″ (A)

- Cut 1 square 3¼″ × 3¼″ (B)

- Cut 4 squares 1⅞″ × 1⅞″. Cut each square in half diagonally once to make 8 triangles (E).

2. From pink fabric, cut 1 square 3¼″ × 3¼″ (B) and 4 squares 1½″ × 1½″ (C).

3. From medium green fabric, cut 2 squares 2⅞″ × 2⅞″. Cut each square in half diagonally once to make 4 triangles (D).

4. From dark blue fabric, cut 2 squares 3¼″ × 3¼″ (B).

5. Sew 2 light beige E triangles to adjacent sides of each pink C square. Press. Sew 1 medium green D triangle to each unit to make 4 block corners. Press. (Refer to page 33, Crowning Glory, Step 4.)

6. Refer to Quick-Pieced Quarter-Square Triangle Variation Units (pages 34 and 35, Dolley Madison's Star, Step 5) to make 4 quick-pieced QST variation units with the light beige, pink, and dark blue B squares.

7. Sew 2 corner units to opposite dark blue sides of a QST variation unit to make the top row. Press. Repeat to make the bottom row.

8. Sew 2 QST variation units to the light beige A square to make the center row. Press.

9. Sew the 3 rows together. Press.

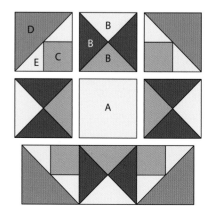

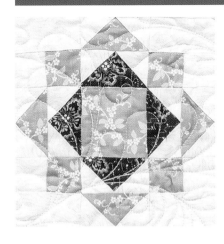

1. From light beige fabric, cut 8 squares 1⅞" × 1⅞" (A), 4 squares 1½" × 1½" (C), and 4 rectangles 1½" × 2½" (D).

2. From medium blue fabric, cut 1 square 3¼" × 3¼" (B), 4 squares 1½" × 1½" (C), and 1 square 2½" × 2½" (E).

3. From red fabric, cut 1 square 3¼" × 3¼" (B).

4. Refer to Quick-Pieced Flying Geese Units (page 26, Corner Star, Step 5) to make 4 quick-pieced Flying Geese units with the medium blue B square and 4 light beige A squares.

5. Refer to Quick-Pieced Flying Geese Units (page 26, Corner Star, Step 5) to make 4 quick-pieced Flying Geese units with the red B square and 4 light beige A squares.

6. Following the assembly diagram for correct alignment, sew each medium blue / light beige Flying Geese unit to a red / light beige Flying Geese unit. Press.

7. Sew each light beige C square to a medium blue C square. Press toward the medium blue fabric. Following the assembly diagram for correct alignment, sew 1 light beige D rectangle to each C/C pair to make 2 corner units and 2 mirror-image corner units. Press.

8. Sew 1 corner unit and 1 mirror-image corner unit to opposite sides of a Flying Geese unit to make the top row. Press. Repeat to make the bottom row.

9. Sew 2 Flying Geese units to opposite sides of the medium blue E square to make the center row. Press.

10. Sew the 3 rows together. Press.

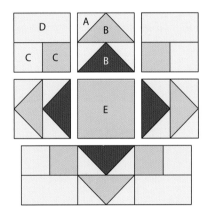

Foundation patterns A and B are on page 102.

1. Make 2 of foundation paper piecing pattern A using dark blue and light beige fabrics.

2. Make 2 of foundation paper piecing pattern B using dark blue and light beige fabrics.

3. Sew each A foundation to a B foundation along the shorter edges to make 2 block halves. Press.

4. Sew the halves together. Press.

Nine-Patch Frame ❧ BLOCK F-9

Foundation patterns A and B are on pages 102 and 103.

1. Make 4 of foundation paper piecing pattern A using light beige, gold, and red fabrics.

2. Make 1 of foundation paper piecing pattern B using light beige and red fabrics.

3. Sewing from point to point and not into the seam allowances, sew 2 A foundations to opposite sides of the B foundation. Press.

4. Using Y-seam construction and sewing in the direction of the arrows, attach 1 A foundation to the B foundation and to the adjacent A foundations. Press.

5. Using Y-seam construction, attach the remaining A foundation to the B foundation and to the adjacent A foundations. Press.

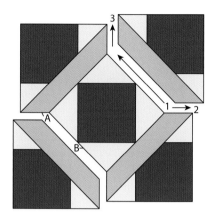

Noon and Night ❧ BLOCK F-10

Foundation patterns A and B are on page 103.

1. Make 2 of foundation paper piecing pattern A using light beige, pink, and medium green fabrics.

2. Make 2 of foundation paper piecing pattern B using light beige, pink, and medium green fabrics.

3. Sew 1 A foundation to a B foundation to make the top row. Press. Repeat to make the bottom row.

4. Sew the 2 rows together. Press.

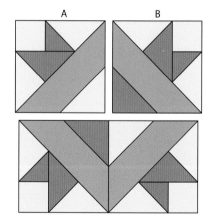

Northumberland Star ✤ Block G-1

1. Make 2 of foundation paper piecing pattern A using dark blue and light beige fabrics.

2. Make 1 of foundation paper piecing pattern B using dark blue, light green, and light beige fabrics.

3. Make 1 of foundation paper piecing pattern C using dark blue and light beige fabrics.

4. Sew the B foundation to the C foundation to make the center row. Press.

5. Sew the A foundations to opposite sides of the center row. Press.

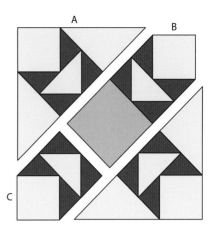

Foundation patterns A, B, and C are on pages 103 and 104.

Old Favorite ✤ Block G-2

2. Make 4 of foundation paper piecing pattern B using light beige and medium green fabrics.

3. Make 4 of foundation paper piecing pattern C using light beige and red fabrics.

4. From medium green fabric, cut 1 square 2″ × 2″ (D).

5. Following the assembly diagram for correct alignment, sew each A foundation to a B foundation. Press.

6. Following the assembly diagram for correct alignment, sew 2 A/B foundation units to opposite sides

of a C foundation to make the top row. Press. Repeat to make the bottom row.

7. Sew 2 C foundations to opposite sides of the medium green D square to make the center row. Press.

8. Sew the 3 rows together. Press.

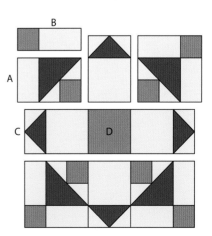

Foundation patterns A, B, and C are on page 104.

1. Make 4 of foundation paper piecing pattern A using light beige, medium green, and red fabrics.

1. From red fabric, cut 1 square 2½″ × 2½″ (A) and 2 squares 3¼″ × 3¼″ (C).

2. From medium blue fabric, cut 4 squares 1½″ × 1½″ (B) and 2 squares 2⅞″ × 2⅞″ (D).

3. From light beige fabric, cut 2 squares 3¼″ × 3¼″ (C) and 2 squares 2⅞″ × 2⅞″ (D).

4. Refer to Quick-Pieced Square-On-Point Units (page 14, Air Castle, Step 4) to make 1 quick-pieced square-on-point unit with the red A square and the medium blue B squares.

NOTE: If you prefer, use the B-3: Christmas Eve foundation paper piecing pattern C (page 97) instead. Adapt colors and adjust your fabric cutting accordingly.

5. Refer to Quick-Pieced Quarter-Square Triangle Units (page 16, Blocks and Stars, Step 5) to make 4 quick-pieced QST units with the light beige C squares and the red C squares.

6. Refer to Quick-Pieced Half-Square Triangle Units (page 14, Air Castle, Step 5) to make 4 quick-pieced HST units with the medium blue D squares and the light beige D squares.

7. Sew 2 HST units to opposite sides of a QST unit to make the top row. Press. Repeat to make the bottom row.

8. Sew 2 QST units to opposite sides of the square-on-point unit to make the center row. Press.

9. Sew the 3 rows together. Press.

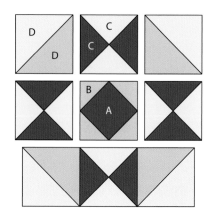

Template patterns A and B are on page 104.

1. From light beige fabric, cut 8 arcs using template A and 8 wedges using template B.

2. From medium green fabric, cut 8 arcs using template A and 8 wedges using template B.

3. Pair each light beige arc A with a medium green wedge B and sew together. Press toward the medium green fabric.

4. Pair each medium green arc A with a light beige wedge B and sew together. Press toward the medium green fabric.

5. Sew the units into 4 rows as shown in the assembly diagram. Press. Sew the 4 rows together. Press.

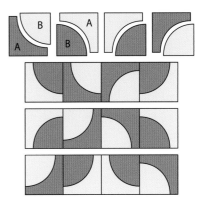

Foundation patterns A, B, and C are on page 105.

1. Make 1 each of foundation paper piecing patterns A, B, and C using light beige and gold fabrics.

2. Sew the B foundation to the A foundation. Press.

3. Sew the C foundation to the A/B foundation unit. Press.

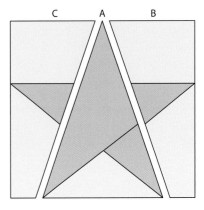

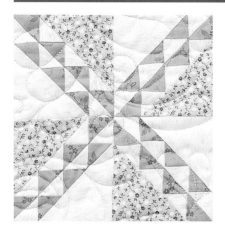

Foundation patterns A and B are on page 105.

1. Make 4 of foundation paper piecing pattern A using light beige, gold, and light green fabrics.

2. Make 4 of foundation paper piecing pattern B using light beige and gold fabrics.

3. Pair each A foundation with a B foundation and sew along the longest edge to make 4 block quarters. Press.

4. Sew the block quarters into 2 rows. Press. Sew the rows together. Press.

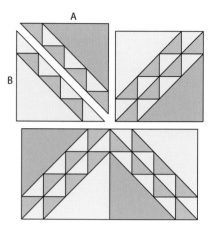

1. From light beige fabric, cut 4 rectangles 1½″ × 2½″ (A) and 4 rectangles 1½″ × 4½″ (B).

2. From medium green fabric, cut 1 square 2½″ × 2½″ (C) and 8 squares 1½″ × 1½″ (D).

3. Sew 2 light beige A rectangles to opposite sides of the medium green C square. Press.

4. Sew 2 medium green D squares to opposite ends of the remaining light beige A rectangles. Press.

5. Sew the strips created in Step 4 to the top and bottom of the block center. Press.

6. Sew 2 light beige B rectangles to opposite sides of the block center. Press.

7. Sew 2 medium green D squares to opposite ends of the remaining light beige B rectangles. Press.

8. Sew the strips created in Step 7 to the top and bottom of the block center. Press.

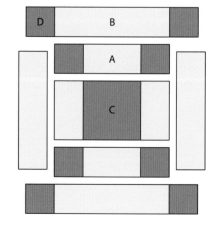

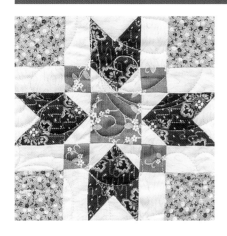

Template pattern A is on page 104.

1. From red fabric, cut 4 rhombuses using template A. Flip the template and cut 4 A Reverse.

2. From medium green fabric, cut 4 squares 1¼″ × 1¼″ (B) and 1 square 2″ × 2″ (C).

3. From pink fabric, cut 4 squares 2″ × 2″ (C).

4. From light beige fabric:

• Cut 8 rectangles 1¼″ × 2″ (D).

• Cut 1 square 2¾″ × 2¾″. Cut the square twice diagonally to make 4 triangles (E).

• Cut 4 squares 1⅝″ × 1⅝″. Cut each square in half once diagonally to make 8 F triangles.

5. Sew each medium green B square to one end of a light beige D rectangle. Press toward the medium green fabric. Sew 1 light beige D rectangle to each pink square. Press toward the pink fabric. Pair a B/D unit with a C/D unit, abut seams, and sew to make 1 block corner. Press. Repeat to make 4.

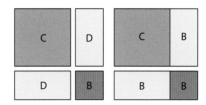

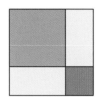

6. Noting correct alignment, sew 1 light beige F triangle to each red A and red A Reverse. Press toward the red fabric on the A Reverse units and the light beige fabric on the A units.

7. Sewing from point to point only and not into the seam allowances, sew each A/F unit to an A Reverse/F unit. Using Y-seam construction, attach a light beige

E triangle to each unit. Press. Make 4 block side units.

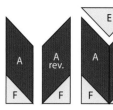

8. Sew 2 block side units to opposite sides of the medium green C square to make the center row, as shown. Press toward the medium green fabric.

9. Sew 2 block corners to opposite sides of each of the remaining block side units to create the top and bottom rows, as shown. Press toward the block corners.

10. Sew the 3 rows together. Press.

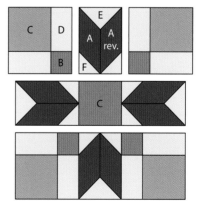

1. From light beige fabric, cut 16 squares 1½″ × 1½″ (A). Draw a diagonal line from corner to corner on the back of each square.

2. From medium blue fabric, cut 4 squares 2½″ × 2½″ (B).

3. From medium green fabric, cut 5 squares 2½″ × 2½″ (C).

4. Matching one corner and aligning adjacent sides, place 1 light beige A square on a medium blue B square, right sides facing. Sew on the drawn line. Trim fabric ¼″ away from the sewn line. Press the seam toward the medium blue

fabric. Repeat with a second light beige A square in an adjacent corner. Repeat with the remaining A and B squares to make 4 identical units.

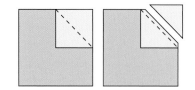

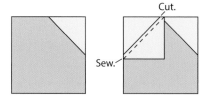

5. Matching one corner and aligning adjacent sides, place 1 light beige A square on a medium green C square. Sew on the drawn line. Trim fabric ¼″ away from the sewn line. Press the seam toward the medium green fabric. Repeat with

a second light beige square in the opposite corner. Press. Repeat to make 4 identical units. (Refer to page 29, Courtyard Quilters, Step 3.)

6. Sew 2 units from Step 5 to a unit from Step 4 to make the top row. Press. Repeat to make the bottom row.

7. Sew 2 units from Step 4 to the remaining medium green C square to make the center row. Press.

8. Sew the 3 rows together. Press.

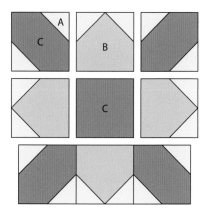

Prairie Star ❧ Block G-10

Foundation pattern A is on page 106.

1. Complete 4 of foundation paper piecing pattern A using red, gold, pink, and light beige fabrics.

2. Sew 2 A foundations together to make the top row. Press. Repeat to make the bottom row.

3. Sew the rows together. Press.

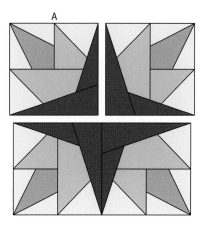

Prickly Poppy ❧ Block H-1

1. From light beige fabric, cut 6 squares 2⅛″ × 2⅛″ (A) and 4 rectangles 1½″ × 2″ (C).

2. From red fabric, cut 2 squares 2⅛″ × 2⅛″ (A).

3. From pink fabric:

• Cut 2 squares 3⅜″ × 3⅜″ Cut each square in half diagonally once to make 4 D triangles.

• Cut 1 square 1½″ × 1½″ (E).

4. From medium green fabric, cut 4 squares 1½″ × 1½″ (E).

5. Refer to Quick-Pieced Half-Square Triangle Units (page 14, Air Castle, Step 5) to make 4 quick-pieced HST units with 2 light beige A squares and 2 red A squares.

6. Cut the remaining 4 light beige A squares in half diagonally once to make 8 B triangles. Sew 2 light beige B triangles to adjacent sides of an HST unit. Press. Sew a pink D triangle to the unit to make 1 block corner. Press. Repeat to make a total of 4 block corners.

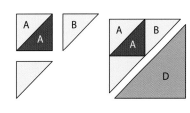

7. Sew a light beige C rectangle to a medium green E square. Press toward the E square. Repeat to make 4.

8. Sew 2 block corners to opposite sides of a C/E unit to make the top row. Press. Repeat to make the bottom row.

9. Sew the remaining C/E units to opposite sides of the pink E square to make the center row. Press.

10. Sew the 3 rows together. Press.

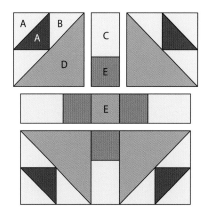

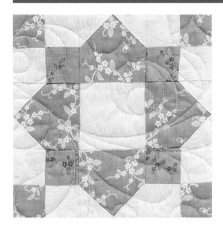

1. From light beige fabric, cut 8 squares 1½″ × 1½″ (A), 1 square 2½″ × 2½″ (B), and 2 strips 1½″ × 8″ (C).

2. From medium blue fabric, cut 4 squares 2½″ × 2½″ (B) and 1 strip 1½″ × 8″ (C).

3. From gold fabric, cut 1 strip 1½″ × 8″ (C).

4. Sew the medium blue C strip and 1 light beige C strip together lengthwise. Press toward the medium blue fabric. Use a rotary cutter to crosscut the strip set into 4 strips 1½″ wide. Repeat with the second light beige C strip and the gold C strip.

5. Pair each medium blue/light beige crosscut strip with a gold/light beige crosscut strip. Sew the strips together to make to make 4 Four-Patch units. Press.

6. Draw a diagonal line from corner to corner on the wrong side of each light beige A square. Matching one corner and aligning adjacent sides, place 1 light beige A square on a medium blue B square, right sides facing. Sew on the drawn line. Trim fabric ¼″ away from the sewn line. Press the seam toward the medium blue fabric. Repeat with a second light beige A square in an adjacent corner. Repeat with the remaining A and B squares to make 4 identical units. (Refer to page 60, Prairie Flower, Step 4.)

7. Sew 2 Four-Patch units to opposite side of 1 unit from Step 6 to make the top row. Press. Repeat for the bottom row.

8. Sew 2 units from Step 6 to the light beige C square to make the center row. Press.

9. Sew the 3 rows together. Press.

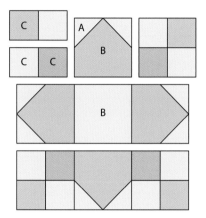

1. From light beige fabric, cut 4 squares 2″ × 2″ (A), 1 square 4¼″ × 4¼″ (B), and 1 square 3½″ × 3½″ (C).

2. From dark blue fabric, cut 4 squares 2″ × 2″ (A) and 4 squares 2⅜″ × 2⅜″ (D).

3. Refer to Quick-Pieced Flying Geese Units (page 26, Corner Star, Step 5) to make 4 quick-pieced Flying Geese units with the dark blue D squares and the light beige B square.

4. Refer to Quick-Pieced Square-On-Point Units (page 14, Air Castle, Step 4) to make 1 quick-pieced square-on-point unit with the light beige C square and the dark blue A squares.

5. Sew 2 light beige A squares to opposite sides of a Flying Geese unit to make the top row. Press. Repeat to make the bottom row.

6. Sew 2 Flying Geese units to opposite sides of the square-on-point unit to make the center row. Press.

7. Sew the 3 rows together. Press

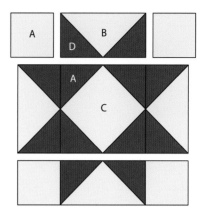

1. From light beige fabric, cut 1 square 2¾″ × 2¾″ (A), 5 squares 2″ × 2″ (C), 4 squares 1¼″ × 1¼″ (D), and 1 square 4¼″ × 4¼″ (E).

2. From pink fabric, cut 4 squares 1⅝″ × 1⅝″ (B).

3. From medium blue fabric, cut 4 squares 2⅜″ × 2⅜″ (F).

4. Refer to Quick-Pieced Flying Geese Units (page 26, Corner Star, Step 5) to make 4 quick-pieced Flying Geese units with the pink B squares and the light beige A square.

5. Refer to Quick-Pieced Flying Geese Units (page 26, Corner Star, Step 5) to make 4 quick-pieced Flying Geese units with the medium blue F squares and the light beige E square.

6. Sew 2 light beige D squares to opposite sides of a pink/light beige Flying Geese unit to make the top row of the central star. Press. Repeat to make the bottom row. Sew 2 pink/light beige Flying Geese units to opposite sides of the light beige C square to make the center row. Press. Sew the 3 rows together to complete the central star.

7. Sew 2 medium blue/light beige Flying Geese units to opposite sides of the central star to make the block center row. Press.

8. Sew 2 light beige C squares to opposite sides of a medium blue/light beige Flying Geese unit to make the block top row. Press. Repeat to make the bottom row.

9. Sew the 3 rows together. Press.

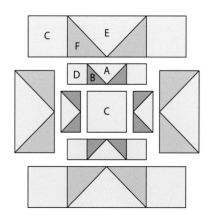

1. From light beige fabric, cut 2 squares 2⅜″ × 2⅜″ (A) and 6 squares 2″ × 2″ (B).

2. From light green fabric, cut 3 squares 2⅜″ × 2⅜″ (A).

3. From medium green fabric, cut 3 squares 2⅜″ × 2⅜″ (A) and 2 squares 2″ × 2″ (B).

4. Refer to Quick-Pieced Half-Square Triangle Units (page 14, Air Castle, Step 5) to make 2 quick-pieced HST units with 1 medium green A square and 1 light beige A square.

5. Refer to Quick-Pieced Half-Square Triangle Units (page 14, Air Castle, Step 5) to make 2 quick-pieced HST units with 1 light green A square and 1 light beige A square.

6. Refer to Quick-Pieced Half-Square Triangle Units (page 14, Air Castle, Step 5) to make 4 quick-pieced HST units with 2 light green A squares and 2 medium green A squares.

7. Following the assembly diagram, arrange the HST units and B squares as shown and sew into 4 rows. Press.

8. Sew the 4 rows together. Press.

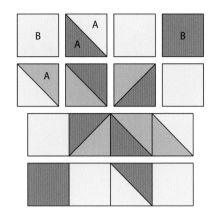

Template patterns B, D, and E are on page 106.

1. From medium green fabric, cut 1 square 1″ × 1″ (A) and 4 of template B.

2. From medium blue fabric, cut 4 squares 1½″ × 1½″ (C) and 4 of template D.

3. From light beige fabric, cut 4 of template E. Cut 4 squares 1⅞″ × 1⅞″. Cut each square in half diagonally once to make 8 triangles (F).

4. Sew 1 medium green B to each medium blue D. Press.

5. Sew 2 light beige E pieces to opposite sides of a B/D unit to make an outer row. Press toward the B/D unit. Repeat to make a second outer row.

6. Sew 2 B/D units to opposite sides of the medium green A square to make the inner row. Press toward the B/D units.

7. Sew 1 outer row to the inner row. Press. Sew the second inner row to the other side. Press.

8. Sew 2 light beige F triangles to adjacent sides of a medium blue C square. Press. Repeat to make 4 block corners.

9. Sew 1 block corner to the long side of each medium green B. Press.

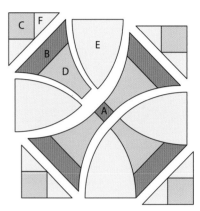

Foundation patterns A and B are on page 106.

1. Make 4 of foundation paper piecing pattern A using light beige and dark blue fabrics.

2. Make 4 of foundation paper piecing pattern B using medium blue and dark blue fabrics.

3. Pair each A foundation with a B foundation and sew along the longest edge to make 4 block quarters. Press.

4. Sew the block quarters into 2 rows. Press. Sew the rows together. Press.

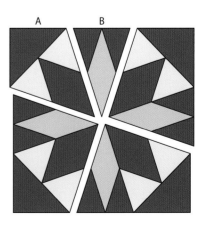

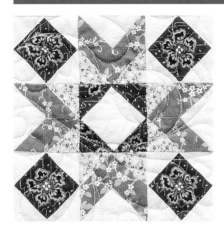

Template pattern D is on page 106.

1. From light beige fabric:

• Cut 1 square 2½″ × 2½″ (A).

• Cut 16 squares 1½″ × 1½″ (B).

• Cut 1 square 3¼″ × 3¼″. Cut the square in half twice diagonally to make 4 triangles (C).

2. From medium green fabric, cut 4 rhombuses using template D. Flip the template and cut 4 D Reverse.

3. From light green fabric, cut 4 squares 1⅞″ × 1⅞″. Cut each square in half diagonally once to make 8 triangles (E).

4. From red fabric, cut 4 squares 2½″ × 2½″ (A) and 4 squares 1½″ × 1½″ (B).

5. Refer to Quick-Pieced Square-On-Point Units (page 14, Air Castle, Step 4) to make 4 quick-pieced square-on-point units with the 4 red A squares and the 16 light beige B squares.

NOTE: If you prefer, use the B-3: Christmas Eve foundation paper piecing pattern C (page 97) instead. Adapt colors and adjust your fabric cutting accordingly.

6. Repeat Step 5 using the light beige A square and 4 red B squares to make 1 square-on-point Reverse unit.

7. Noting the correct alignment, sew 1 light green E triangle to each medium green D and D Reverse. Press toward the medium green fabric for the D Reverse units and the light beige fabric for the D units. Press. Make 4 block side units.

8. Sewing from point to point only and not into the seam allowances, sew a D/E unit to a D Reverse/E unit, as shown. Using Y-seam construction, attach a light beige

C triangle to each unit. Press. Repeat to make 4 block side units.

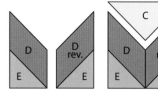

9. Sew 2 square-on-point units to opposite sides of a block side unit to make the top row. Press. Repeat to make the bottom row.

10. Sew 2 block side units to opposite sides of the square-on-point Reverse unit to make the center row. Press.

11. Sew the 3 rows together. Press.

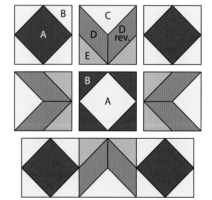

Sawmill ❧ Block H-9

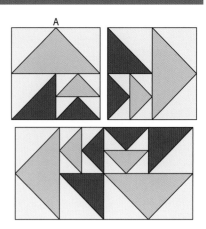

Foundation pattern A is on page 106.

1. Make 4 of foundation paper piecing pattern A using dark blue, gold, and light beige fabrics.

2. Following the assembly diagram for correct alignment, sew the A foundations into pairs to make 2 rows. Press.

3. Sew the 2 rows together. Press.

Scotch Squares ❧ Block H-10

Template pattern D is on page 106.

1. From light beige fabric:

• Cut 6 squares 2⅜″ × 2⅜″ (A). Cut 4 A squares in half diagonally once to make 8 triangles (B).

• Cut 1 square 2¾″ × 2¾″. Cut the square in half diagonally twice to make 4 triangles (C).

2. From medium blue fabric:

• Cut 2 squares 2⅜″ × 2⅜″ (A).

• Cut 1 square 2¾″ × 2¾″. Cut the square in half diagonally twice to make 4 triangles (C).

• Cut 1 square 2⅝″ × 2⅝″ (E).

3. From red fabric, cut 4 rectangles using template D.

4. Refer to Quick-Pieced Half-Square Triangle Units (page 14, Air Castle, Step 5) to make 4 quick-pieced HST units with 2 light beige A squares and 2 medium blue A squares.

5. Sew 2 light beige B triangles to adjacent medium blue edges of an HST unit. Press. Repeat to make 4 block corners.

6. Sew each light beige C triangle to a medium blue C triangle along the longest edge. Press. Sew 2 C/C units to opposite sides of a red D rectangle. Press. Repeat to make a second unit.

7. Sew 2 red D rectangles to opposite sides of the medium blue E square. Press.

8. Sew the 2 units created in Step 6 to opposite sides of the unit created in Step 7 to make the block center. Press.

9. Sew 2 block corners to opposite sides of the block center. Press. Sew the other 2 block corners to the remaining sides. Press.

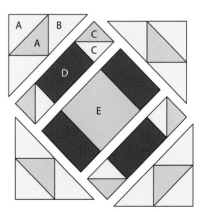

1. From light beige fabric, cut 8 squares 1½″ × 1½″ (A) and 2 strips 1½″ × 8″ (C).

2. From gold fabric, cut 4 squares 2½″ × 2½″ (B)

3. From medium green fabric, cut 2 strips 1½″ × 8″ (C).

4. From dark blue fabric, cut 2 strips 1½″ × 8″ (C).

5. Sew a dark blue C strip and a light beige C strip together lengthwise. Press toward the dark blue fabric. Use a rotary cutter to crosscut the strip set into 4 strips 1½″ wide. Sew the strips together in pairs to make 2 dark blue/light beige Four-Patch units. Press.

6. Repeat the previous step using the second light beige C strip and a medium green C strip to make 2 medium green/light beige Four-Patch units. Press. Repeat with the remaining dark blue C and medium green C strips to make 1 dark blue/medium green Four-Patch unit. Press.

7. Draw 1 diagonal line from corner to corner on the wrong side of each light beige A square. Matching one corner and aligning adjacent sides, place 1 light beige A square on a gold B square, right sides facing. Sew on the drawn line. Trim fabric ¼″ away from the sewn line. Press the seam toward the gold fabric. Repeat with a second light beige A square in an adjacent corner. Press. Repeat with the remaining A and B squares to make 4 identical units. (Refer to page 60, Prairie Flower, Step 4.)

8. Noting correct color placement, sew 2 Four-Patch units to opposite sides of 1 unit from Step 7 to make the top row. Press. Repeat for the bottom row.

9. Sew 2 units from Step 7 to opposite sides of the dark blue/medium green Four-Patch unit to make the center row. Press.

10. Sew the 3 rows together. Press.

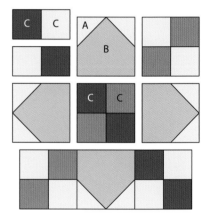

Template patterns A, B, C, D, and E and the appliqué placement diagram are on page 107.

1. From light beige fabric, cut 1 square 6½″ × 6½″ (F). Fold the square in half vertically, horizontally, and diagonally both ways, pressing after each fold to mark the appliqué placement lines.

> **NOTE:** You can also cut the square larger and trim to size after sewing the appliqué pieces in place, if desired.

2. From red fabric, cut 16 of the bud template A and 1 of the flower center template E, adding the required seam allowance for your preferred appliqué method.

3. From pink fabric, cut 16 of the petal template B and 1 of the small flower template D, adding the required seam allowance for your preferred appliqué method.

4. From medium green fabric, cut 1 of the large flower template C, adding the required seam allowance for your preferred appliqué method.

5. Appliqué the red flower center E to the pink small flower D. Appliqué the D/E unit to the medium green large flower C.

> **NOTE:** You can use reverse appliqué for the D/E pair if preferred.

6. Following the appliqué placement diagram (page 107), appliqué the 8 inner red buds to the light beige F square. Appliqué the pink B petals on top of the inner red buds. Appliqué the C/D/E flower in place on the light beige F square, covering the inner tips of the pink B petals. Appliqué the outer A buds between the inner buds to the light beige F square.

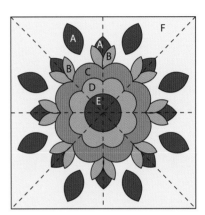

Foundation pattern A is on page 108.

1. Make 4 of foundation paper piecing pattern A using light beige, medium green, light green, pink, and red fabrics.

2. Following the assembly diagram for correct alignment, sew the A foundations into pairs to make 2 rows. Press.

3. Sew the rows together. Press.

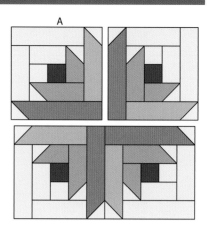

Spinning Wheel ❧ BLOCK I-4

Template pattern D is on page 108.

1. From light beige fabric:

• Cut 2 squares 2⅞″ × 2⅞″ (A).

• Cut 8 squares 1⅞″ × 1⅞″. Cut each square in half diagonally once to make 16 triangles (B).

• Cut 8 squares using template D.

2. From red fabric, cut 2 squares 2⅞″ × 2⅞″ (A) and 1 square 2½″ × 2½″ (C).

3. From pink fabric, cut 8 squares using template D.

4. Sew each light beige D square to a pink D square. Press. Sew the units together in pairs to make 4 Four-Patch units. Press.

5. Sew 2 light beige B triangles to opposite sides of 1 Four-Patch unit. Press. Sew 2 light beige B triangles to the remaining sides. Press. Repeat to make 4 units.

6. Refer to Quick-Pieced Half-Square Triangle Units (page 14, Air Castle, Step 5) to make 4 quick-pieced HST units with the red A squares and the light beige A squares.

7. Sew 2 HST units to opposite sides of a unit created in Step 5 to make the top row. Press. Repeat to make the bottom row.

8. Sew the remaining 2 HST units created in Step 5 to opposite sides of the red C square to make the center row. Press.

9. Sew the 3 rows together. Press.

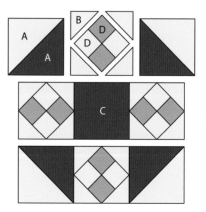

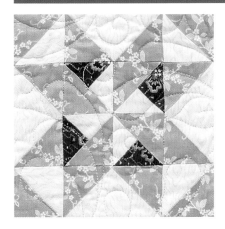

1. From light beige fabric:

• Cut 1 square 2¾″ × 2¾″. Cut the square in half diagonally twice to make 4 A triangles.

• Cut 1 square 4¼″ × 4¼″ (B)

• Cut 2 squares 2⅜″ × 2⅜″ (D)

2. From medium blue fabric, cut 8 squares 2⅜″ × 2⅜″ (D). Cut 2 D squares in half diagonally once to make 4 C triangles.

3. From red fabric, cut 1 square 2¾″ × 2¾″. Cut the square in half diagonally twice to make 4 A triangles.

4. Refer to Quick-Pieced Flying Geese Units (page 26, Corner Star, Step 5) to make 4 quick-pieced Flying Geese units with the medium blue D squares and the light beige B square.

5. Refer to Quick-Pieced Half-Square Triangle Units (page 14, Air Castle, Step 5) to make 4 quick-pieced HST units with the medium blue D squares and the light beige D squares.

6. Noting correct alignment, sew 1 light beige A triangle to each red A triangle and sew along the short edge. Press toward the red fabric.

7. Sew 1 medium blue C triangle to each A/A triangle pair. Press toward the medium blue fabric.

8. Sew the units created in Step 7 together in pairs to make 2 rows. Press toward the medium blue fabric. Sew the rows together to make the central pinwheel unit. Press.

9. Noting correct alignment, sew 2 HST units to opposite sides of a Flying Geese unit to make the top row. Press. Repeat to make the bottom row.

10. Sew 2 Flying Geese units to opposite sides of the central pinwheel unit to make the center row. Press.

11. Sew the 3 rows together. Press.

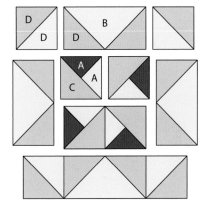

1. From light beige fabric, cut 4 squares 1⅞″ × 1⅞″ (A) and 2 squares 2⅞″ × 2⅞″ (C).

2. From light green fabric, cut 1 square 3¼″ × 3¼″ (B).

3. From gold fabric, cut 2 squares 2⅞″ × 2⅞″ (C) and 1 square 2½″ × 2½″ (D).

4. From dark blue fabric, cut 4 squares 1⅞″ × 1⅞″ (A) and 1 square 3¼″ × 3¼″ (B).

5. Refer to Quick-Pieced Flying Geese Units (page 26, Corner Star, Step 5) to make 4 quick-pieced Flying Geese units with the dark blue A squares and the light green B square.

6. Refer to Quick-Pieced Flying Geese Units (page 26, Corner Star, Step 5) to make 4 quick-pieced Flying Geese units with the light beige A squares and the dark blue B square.

7. Refer to Quick-Pieced Half-Square Triangle Units (page 14, Air Castle, Step 5) to make 4 quick-pieced HST units with the gold C squares and the light beige C squares.

8. Following the assembly diagram for correct alignment, sew 1 dark blue/light beige Flying Geese unit to 1 light green/dark blue Flying Geese unit. Press. Repeat to make 4.

9. Sew 2 HST units to opposite sides of a Flying Geese pair to make the top row. Press. Repeat to make the bottom row.

10. Sew 2 Flying Geese units to opposite sides of the gold D square to make the center row. Press.

11. Sew the 3 rows together. Press.

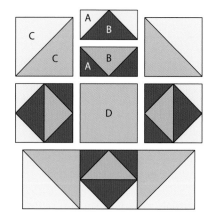

Template pattern D is on page 107.

1. From light beige fabric:

• Cut 4 squares 1½″ × 1½″ (B).

• Cut 4 rectangles 1½″ × 2½″ E).

• Cut 2 squares 2⅞″ × 2⅞″. Cut each square in half diagonally once to make 4 triangles (G).

2. From red fabric:

• Cut 1 square 2½″ × 2½″ (A).

• Cut 1 square 3¼″ × 3¼″. Cut in half diagonally twice to make 4 triangles (C).

• Cut 4 squares 1⅞″ × 1⅞″. Cut each square in half diagonally once to make 8 triangles (F).

3. Cut 4 of template D from medium blue fabric. Flip the template and cut 4 D Reverse.

4. Refer to Quick-Pieced Square-On-Point Units (page 14, Air Castle, Step 4) to make 1 quick-pieced square-on-point unit with the red A square and the light beige B squares.

NOTE: If you prefer, use the B-3: Christmas Eve foundation paper piecing pattern C (page 97) instead. Adjust your fabric cutting accordingly.

5. Sew 1 D and 1 D Reverse to adjacent short sides of a red C triangle. Press. Repeat to make 4.

6. Sewing from point to point and not into the seam allowances, sew 1 D/C/D Reverse unit to the square-on-point unit. Sew another D/C/D Reverse unit to the opposite side. Using Y-seam construction, sew the other 2 D/C/D Reverse units to the remaining sides. Sew in the direction of the arrows. Press.

7. Sew 2 red F triangles to opposite sides of each light beige E rectangle. Press.

8. Sew 2 F/E/F units to opposite sides of the unit created in Step 6. Press. Sew the remaining F/E/F units to the other sides. Press.

9. Sew the light beige G triangles to the corners of the block. Press.

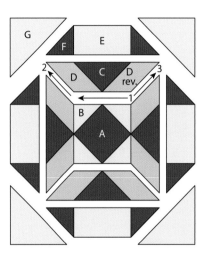

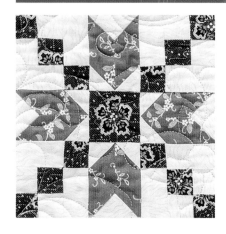

Template pattern A is on page 107.

1. From medium green fabric, cut 4 rhombuses using template A. Flip the template and cut 4 A Reverse.

2. From dark blue fabric, cut 1 strip 1¼″ × 12″ (G), 4 squares 1¼″ × 1¼″ (B), and 1 square 2″ × 2″ (C).

3. From light beige fabric:

• Cut 1 strip 1¼″ × 12″ (G).

• Cut 8 rectangles 1¼″ × 2″ (D).

• Cut 1 square 2¾″ × 2¾″. Cut the square twice diagonally to make 4 triangles (E).

• Cut 4 squares 1⅝″ × 1⅝″. Cut each square in half once diagonally to make 8 F triangles.

4. Sew the dark blue strip and the light beige strip together lengthwise. Press toward the dark blue fabric. Use a rotary cutter to crosscut the strip set into 8 strips 1¼″ wide. Sew the strips in pairs to make 4 Four-Patch units.

5. Sew a light beige D rectangle to each Four-Patch. Sew a dark blue B square to the end of each remaining light beige D rectangle. Sew 1 square/rectangle unit to each Four-Patch to create a block corner. Make 4.

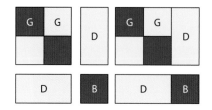

6. Noting correct alignment, sew 1 light beige F triangle to each medium green A and medium green A Reverse. Press toward the medium green fabric for the A Reverse units and toward the light beige fabric for the A units.

7. Sewing from point to point only, sew each A/F unit to an A Reverse/F unit. Using Y-seam construction, attach a light beige E triangle to each unit. Press. Repeat to make 4 block side units.

8. Sew 2 block side units to opposite sides of the dark blue C square to make the center row. Press toward the dark blue fabric.

9. Sew 2 block corners to opposite sides of each of the remaining block side units to create the top and bottom rows. Press toward the block corners.

10. Sew the 3 rows together. Press.

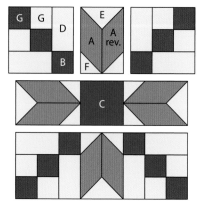

Template patterns A, B, C, D, E, and F and the appliqué placement diagram are on page 108.

1. From light beige fabric, cut 1 square 6½″ × 6½″ (G). Fold the square in half vertically, horizontally, and diagonally both ways, pressing after each fold to mark the appliqué placement lines.

NOTE: You can also cut the square larger and trim to size after sewing the appliqué pieces in place, if desired.

2. From pink fabric, cut 8 of the bud template A, adding the required seam allowance for your preferred appliqué method.

3. From medium green fabric, cut 8 stems using template B and 16 leaves using template F, adding the required seam allowance for your preferred appliqué method. Cut a bias strip ¼″ × 10″ for the C vine.

NOTE: If you prefer, cut a circle using the appliqué placement diagram as a template, or you can embroider the vine.

4. From red fabric, cut 4 flowers using template D, adding the required seam allowance for your preferred appliqué method.

5. From gold fabric, cut 4 flower centers using template E, adding the required seam allowance for your preferred appliqué method.

NOTE: You can use reverse appliqué when sewing the D and E pieces. Adjust template and fabric cutting accordingly.

6. Following the appliqué placement diagram (page 108), appliqué the pieces to the light beige G square in the following order: A buds, B stems, C bias vine, D flowers, E flower centers, F leaves.

1. From light beige fabric, cut 10 squares 1⅞″ × 1⅞″ (A), 4 rectangles 1½″ × 2½″ (C), and 1 square 2½″ × 2½″ (D).

2. From gold fabric, cut 2 squares 1⅞″ × 1⅞″ (A).

3. From red fabric, cut 4 squares 1⅞″ × 1⅞″ (A) and 1 square 3¼″ × 3¼″ (B).

4. From medium blue fabric, cut 4 squares 1½″ × 1½″ (E).

5. Refer to Quick-Pieced Half-Square Triangle Units (page 14, Air Castle, Step 5) to make 4 quick-pieced HST units with 2 gold A squares and 2 light beige A squares.

6. Refer to Quick-Pieced Half-Square Triangle Units (page 14, Air Castle, Step 5) to make 8 quick-pieced HST units with 4 red A squares and 4 light beige A squares.

7. Refer to Quick-Pieced Flying Geese Units (page 26, Corner Star, Step 5) to make 4 quick-pieced Flying Geese units with the red B square and 4 light beige A squares.

8. Sew 1 light beige C rectangle to each Flying Geese unit to make 4 block side units. Press.

9. Sew a gold/light beige HST unit to a red/light beige HST unit, as shown. Press. Repeat to make 4.

10. Sew a medium blue E square to a red/light beige HST unit, as shown. Press. Repeat to make 4.

11. Sew a unit made in Step 9 to a unit made in Step 10, as shown. Press. Repeat to make 4 block corners.

12. Sew 2 block corners to opposite sides of a block side unit to make the top row, as shown. Press. Repeat to make the bottom row.

13. Sew 2 block side units to opposite sides of the light beige D square to make the center row. Press.

14. Sew the 3 rows together. Press.

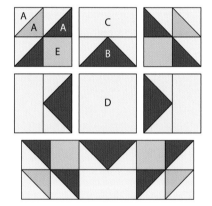

Swamp Rose ✿ BLOCK J-1

Foundation patterns A and B are on pages 108 and 109. Foundation pattern C is on page 110.

1. Make 4 of foundation paper piecing pattern A using medium green and light beige fabrics.

2. Make 4 of foundation paper piecing pattern B using red, medium green, and light beige fabrics.

3. Make 1 of foundation paper piecing pattern C using red and light beige fabrics as they appear in the block assembly diagram.

4. Sew 2 A foundations to opposite sides of a B foundation to make the top row. Press. Repeat to make the bottom row.

5. Sew 2 B foundations to opposite sides of the C foundation to make the center row. Press.

6. Sew the 3 rows together. Press.

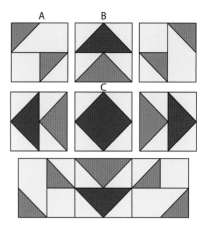

Treasure Chest ✿ BLOCK J-2

Foundation patterns A, B, and C are on page 109.

1. Make 2 of foundation paper piecing pattern A from light beige, dark blue, gold, and light green fabrics.

2. Make 1 of foundation paper piecing pattern B from light beige, dark blue, gold, and light green fabrics.

3. Make 1 of foundation paper piecing pattern C from light beige, dark blue, gold, and light green fabrics.

4. Sew the B foundation to the C foundation to make the center row. Press.

5. Sew 2 A foundations to opposite sides of the center row. Press.

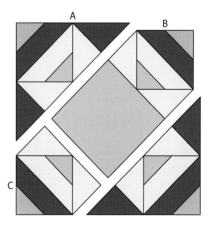

Tulip Wreath ❧ BLOCK J-3

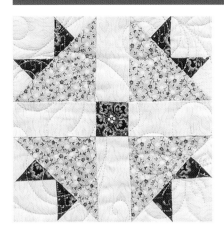

Foundation pattern A is on page 110.

1. From light beige fabric, cut 4 rectangles 1½″ × 3″ (B).

2. From red fabric, cut 1 square 1½″ × 1½″ (C).

3. Make 4 of foundation paper piecing pattern A using red, light green, and light beige fabrics.

4. Sew 2 A foundations to opposite sides of a light beige B rectangle to make the top row. Press. Repeat to make the bottom row.

5. Sew 2 light beige B rectangles to opposite sides of the red C square to make the center row. Press.

6. Sew the 3 rows together. Press.

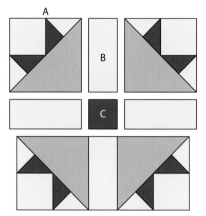

Union Squares ❧ BLOCK J-4

Template pattern A is on page 110.

1. From medium blue fabric, cut 5 squares using template A.

2. From dark blue fabric, cut 4 squares using template A and 4 squares 2″ × 2″ (B).

3. From light beige fabric, cut 4 squares 2⅜″ × 2⅜″. Cut each square in half diagonally once to make 8 triangles (C).

4. Sew 2 medium blue A squares to opposite sides of a dark blue A square. Press. Repeat to make a second identical row. Sew 2 dark blue A squares to opposite sides of a medium blue A square. Press. Sew the 3 rows together to make the central Nine-Patch unit. Press.

5. Sew 2 light beige C triangles to adjacent sides of a dark blue B square. Press. Repeat to make 4 block corners.

6. Sew 2 block corners to opposite sides of the central Nine-Patch unit. Press. Sew the other 2 block corners to the remaining sides. Press.

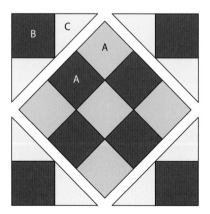

Template patterns A, B, and C are on page 110.

1. From light beige fabric, cut 4 squares using template A, 4 triangles using template B, and 16 rhombuses using template C.

2. Using template C, cut 8 rhombuses from gold fabric and 8 from red fabric.

3. Sew a light beige C to each red C. Press toward the red fabric. Sew a light beige C to each gold C. Press toward the gold fabric.

4. Pair each light beige/red C/C unit with a light beige/gold C/C unit and sew together to make 8 star points.

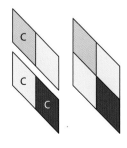

5. Sewing from point to point and not into the seam allowance, sew 2 star points together. Press. Using Y-seam construction, attach a light beige B triangle to the unit. Press. Repeat to make 4.

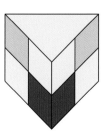

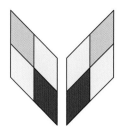

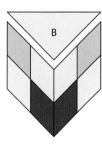

6. Sewing from point to point, attach 1 light beige A square to each unit created in Step 5. Press. Join the units together in pairs to make 2 block halves. Sew in the direction of the arrows. Press.

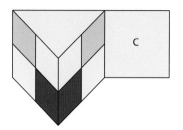

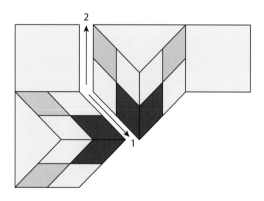

7. Sewing from point to point in the direction of the arrows, sew the block halves together. Press.

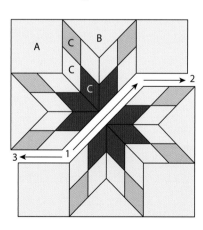

1. From light beige fabric, cut 2 squares 2⅞″ × 2⅞″ (A) and 1 strip 1½″ × 17″ (B).

2. From medium green fabric, cut 2 squares 2⅞″ × 2⅞″ (A) and 1 strip 1½″ × 17″ (B).

3. Refer to Quick-Pieced Half-Square Triangle Units (page 14, Air Castle, Step 5) to make 4 quick-pieced HST units with the medium green A squares and the light beige A squares.

4. Sew the medium green B strip and the light beige B strip together lengthwise. Press toward the medium green fabric. Use a rotary cutter to crosscut the strip set into 10 strips 1½″ wide. Sew the strips together in pairs to make 5 Four-Patch units. Press.

5. Following the assembly diagram for correct alignment, sew 2 Four-Patch units to opposite sides of an HST unit to make the top row. Press. Repeat to make the bottom row.

6. Following the assembly diagram for correct alignment, sew 2 HST units to opposite sides of the remaining Four-Patch unit to make the center row. Press.

7. Sew the 3 rows together. Press.

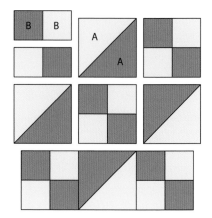

Template patterns C and E are on page 110.

1. From light beige fabric:

• Cut 8 squares 1½″ × 1½″ (A).

• Cut 2 squares 1⅞″ × 1⅞″ (B).

• Cut 4 squares using template C.

• Cut 1 square 3¼″ × 3¼″. Cut the square in half twice diagonally to make 4 D triangles.

2. From medium green fabric, cut 4 of template E. Flip over the template and cut 4 E Reverse.

3. From pink fabric:

• Cut 4 squares 1⅞″ × 1⅞″ (B). Cut 2 B squares in half diagonally to make 4 triangles (F).

• Cut 1 square using template C.

4. Refer to Quick-Pieced Half-Square Triangle Units (page 14, Air Castle, Step 5) to make 4 quick-pieced HST units with 2 pink B squares and 2 light beige B squares.

5. Noting correct alignment, sew 1 light beige A square to an HST unit. Press. Repeat to make 4. Sew a pink F triangle to a light beige A square. Press. Repeat to make 4. Sew each HST/A unit to an A/F unit. Press. Repeat to make 4 block corners.

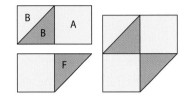

6. Sewing from point to point, sew each medium green E piece to a medium green E Reverse along the short side. Press. Using Y-seam construction, attach 1 light beige D triangle to the units. Press. Make 4.

7. Sewing from point to point, sew 2 of the units created in Step 6 to opposite sides of a light beige C square. Press. Repeat to make 2.

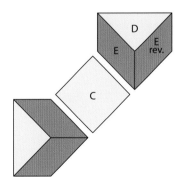

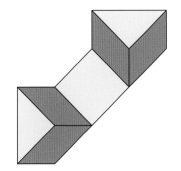

8. Sew the 2 remaining light beige C squares to opposite sides of the pink C square. Press.

9. Sewing from point to point, sew the 2 units created in Step 7 to the unit created in Step 8. Press.

10. Using Y-seam construction, sew the block corners to the unit created in Step 9. Press.

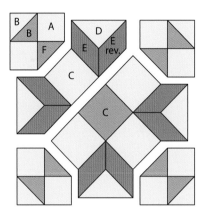

Template patterns A, B, and C are on page 110.

1. From light beige fabric:

• Cut 4 triangles using template A.

• Cut 4 triangles using template B. Flip the template over and cut 4 B Reverse triangles.

2. From red fabric, cut 4 triangles using template A and 4 triangles using template C.

3. From medium green fabric, cut 4 triangles using template A.

4. Pair each medium green A triangle with a light beige A triangle and sew along the longest edge. Press toward the medium green fabric. Sew 2 A/A triangle pairs together to make half of the central octagon. Press. Repeat to make the second half. Sew the halves together to make the central octagon. Press.

5. Sew a red C triangle to the end of each medium green A triangle. Press.

6. Sew 1 light beige B triangle and 1 light beige B Reverse triangle to each side of a red A triangle to make a block corner. Press. Repeat to make 4 block corners.

7. Sew 2 block corners to opposite sides of the unit created in Step 5. Press. Sew the remaining 2 block corners to the other sides. Press.

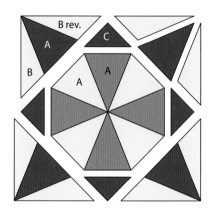

1. From light beige fabric, cut 4 squares 2″ × 2″ (A).

2. Cut 1 square 2″ × 2″ (A) and 1 rectangle 2″ × 3½″ (B) each from gold, medium green, red, and dark blue fabrics.

3. Sew each light beige A square to an A square in a contrasting fabric. Press toward the darker fabric.

4. Arrange the block segments as shown in the assembly diagram and sew into 2 rows. Press. Sew the rows together. Press.

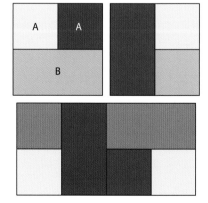

Template pattern A is on page 110.

1. From light beige fabric:

• Cut 2 squares 2¾″ × 2¾″. Cut each square in half diagonally twice to make 8 B triangles.

• Cut 4 squares 2″ × 2″ (C).

2. From medium blue fabric, cut 4 squares using template A and 1 square 2⅝″ × 2⅝″ (D).

3. From medium green fabric, cut 2 squares 2⅜″ × 2⅜″. Cut each square in half diagonally once to make 4 E triangles.

4. From dark blue fabric, cut 1 square 4¼″ × 4¼″. Cut the square in half diagonally twice to make 4 F triangles.

5. Sew 2 light beige B triangles to adjacent sides of each medium blue A square. Press.

6. Following the assembly diagram for correct alignment, sew 1 medium green E triangle to each light beige C square. Press.

7. Sew 1 dark blue F triangle to each of the units created in Step 6. Press.

8. Sew 2 B/B/A units to opposite sides of a C/E/F unit to make the top row. Press. Repeat to make the bottom row.

9. Sew 2 C/E/F units to opposite sides of the medium blue D square to make the center row. Press.

10. Sew the 3 rows together. Press.

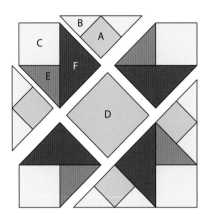

General Instructions

Sashing and Borders

CUTTING

Yardage is calculated assuming a 42″ usable width of fabric.

Light beige:

• Cut 4 strips 6½″ × width of fabric. Subcut into 90 vertical sashing pieces 1½″ × 6½″

• Cut 9 strips 1½″ × 69½″ on the length of fabric for horizontal sashing pieces

Option: Cut 18 strips 1½″ × width of fabric. Sew diagonally end to end.
Subcut into 9 sashing strips 1½″ × 69½″.

• Cut 2 strips 1½″ × 69½″ on the length of fabric for side inner borders

• Cut 2 strips 1½″ × 71½″on the length of fabric for top and bottom inner borders

Option: Cut 8 strips 1½″ × width of fabric. Sew diagonally end to end.
Subcut into 2 inner border strips 1½″ × 69½″ and 2 inner border strips 71½″.

Multicolor floral:

• Cut 2 strips 10″ × 71½″ on the lengthwise grain for the side outer border

• Cut 2 strips 10″ × 90½″ on the lengthwise grain for the top and bottom outer border

Option: Cut 11 strips 10″ × width of fabric. Sew diagonally end to end.
Subcut into 2 outer border strips 10″ × 71½″ and 2 outer border strips 10″ × 90½″.

Note: The width of your outer border will vary according to the width of the stripe or other design in your fabric. Cut according to the most attractive width, remembering to add a ¼″ seam allowance to both long edges. Substitute a floral or other print if desired.

Quilt Assembly

1. Arrange the sampler blocks in 10 rows of 10 blocks. Sew 9 vertical sashing strips 1½″ × 6½″ between the blocks for each row. Press toward the sashing strips.

2. Sew the horizontal sashing pieces 1½″ × 69½″ between the rows. Press toward the sashing rows.

3. Sew the 1½″ × 69½″ inner border pieces to the side edges. Press to the inner border. Sew the 1½″ × 71½ inner border pieces to the top and bottom edges. Press toward the inner border.

4. Sew the 10″ × 71½″ outer border pieces to the side edges. Press toward the outer border. Sew the 10″ × 90½″ outer border pieces to the top and bottom edges. Press toward the outer border.

5. Refer to your favorite basic quilting book to layer the quilt top, backing, and batting. Baste. Quilt as desired. Attach a hanging sleeve and bind.

A-1		A-2	A-3	A-4	A-5	A-6	A-7	A-8	A-9	A-10

B-1	B-2	B-3	B-4	B-5	B-6	B-7	B-8	B-9	B-10
C-1	C-2	C-3	C-4	C-5	C-6	C-7	C-8	C-9	C-10
D-1	D-2	D-3	D-4	D-5	D-6	D-7	D-8	D-9	D-10
E-1	E-2	E-3	E-4	E-5	E-6	E-7	E-8	E-9	E-10
F-1	F-2	F-3	F-4	F-5	F-6	F-7	F-8	F-9	F-10
G-1	G-2	G-3	G-4	G-5	G-6	G-7	G-8	G-9	G-10
H-1	H-2	H-3	H-4	H-5	H-6	H-7	H-8	H-9	H-10
I-1	I-2	I-3	I-4	I-5	I-6	I-7	I-8	I-9	I-10
J-1	J-2	J-3	J-4	J-5	J-6	J-7	J-8	J-9	J-10

Quilt assembly

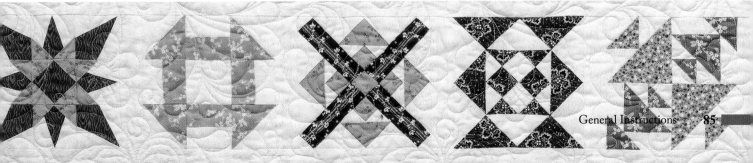

The Gallery

HARRIET'S SAMPLER 2019 ❧ 83″ × 83″, pieced and appliquéd by Shelley Stevens, machine quilted by Joanne Beard, 2019. The "Winding Ways Quilt Collection" and "Elizabeth's Collection" fabrics by Jennifer Chiaverini used in this quilt were provided by Red Rooster Fabrics.

SCRAPPY HARRIET ❧ 76˝ × 76˝, pieced and appliquéd by Geraldine Neidenbach, machine quilted by Sue Vollbrecht, 2019

HARRIET'S EMERALD JOURNEY ❧ 55½″ × 73″, pieced by Cecile Flegg, machine quilted by Kim Caskey, 2019

CHRISTMAS BELLS 64″ × 64″, pieced and appliquéd by Jennifer Chiaverini, machine quilted by Sue Vollbrecht, 2019. The "Christmas Bells Collection" fabrics by Jennifer Chiaverini used in this quilt were provided by Red Rooster Fabrics.

BORN OUT ✂ 37″ × 47½″, pieced by Dana Mosling, machine quilted by Heather Matanock, 2019

HOLLY JOLLY HARRIET ❄ 63″ × 80″, pieced by Jennifer Chiaverini, machine quilted by Sue Vollbrecht, 2019

This quilt demonstrates how beautifully blocks from *Harriet's Journey*, *Sylvia's Bridal Sampler*, and *Loyal Union Sampler* work together. To make this quilt, make 25 sampler blocks and arrange them on-point, alternating with 48 G-7 Pennsylvania blocks (page 58).

PAISLEY ROSE 31″ × 33″, pieced by Geraldine Neidenbach, machine quilted by Sue Vollbrecht, 2019

LUAU ✿ 51″ × 18″, pieced by Heather Neidenbach, machine quilted by Sue Vollbrecht, 2019

INTROSPECTION ❖ 37″ × 43½″, pieced and machine quilted by Cassandra Slocum, 2019

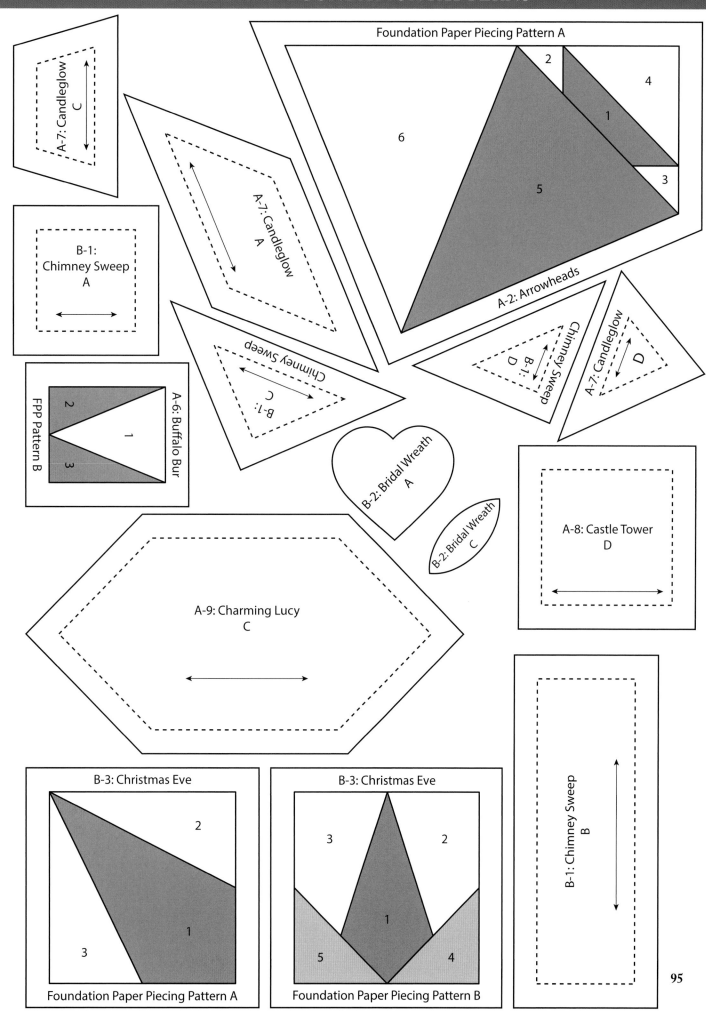

A-7: Candleglow
C

A-7: Candleglow
A

B-1:
Chimney Sweep
A

Chimney Sweep
C
B-1:

FPP Pattern B

A-6: Buffalo Bur

Foundation Paper Piecing Pattern A

2

4

1

3

6

5

A-2: Arrowheads

Chimney Sweep
B-1:
D

A-7: Candleglow
D

B-2: Bridal Wreath
A

B-2: Bridal Wreath
C

A-8: Castle Tower
D

A-9: Charming Lucy
C

B-3: Christmas Eve

2

1

3

Foundation Paper Piecing Pattern A

B-3: Christmas Eve

3

2

1

5

4

Foundation Paper Piecing Pattern B

B-1: Chimney Sweep
B

95

B-2: Bridal Wreath
Appliqué Placement

B-5: City of Spindles

Foundation Paper Piecing Pattern C

Foundation Paper Piecing Pattern A

B-5: City of Spindles

B-5: City of Spindles

Foundation Paper Piecing Pattern B

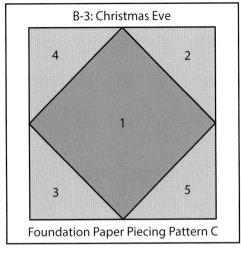

B-3: Christmas Eve

4   2

1

3   5

Foundation Paper Piecing Pattern C

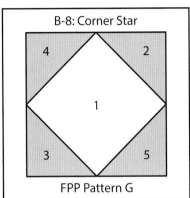

B-8: Corner Star

4   2

1

3   5

FPP Pattern G

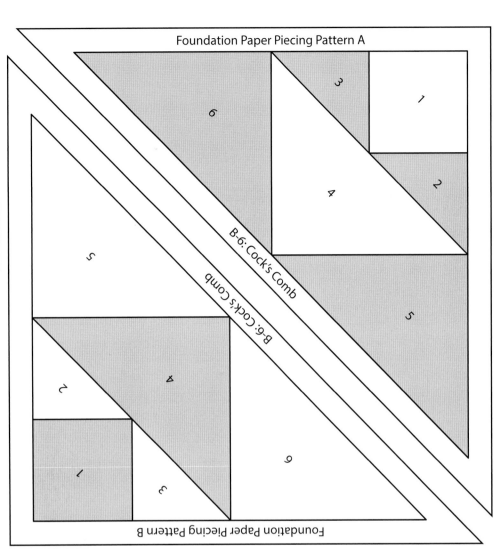

Foundation Paper Piecing Pattern A

B-6: Cock's Comb

B-6: Cock's Comb

Foundation Paper Piecing Pattern B

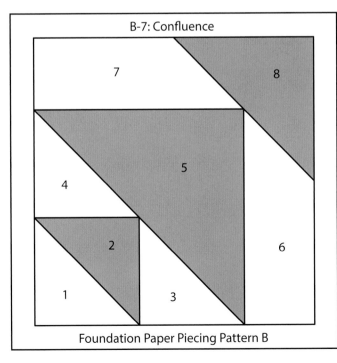

B-7: Confluence

7   8

5

4

2

1   3   6

Foundation Paper Piecing Pattern B

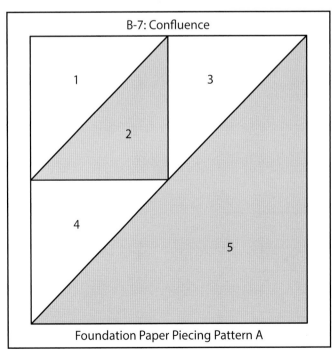

B-7: Confluence

1   3

2

4

5

Foundation Paper Piecing Pattern A

B-9: Oak Leaves
Appliqué Placement

C-2: D

Cross and Chains

B-10:
County Fair
E

B-9:
Oak Leaves
A

B-9:
Oak Leaves
B

B-9:
Oak Leaves
C

C-7: Double Pinwheel

Foundation Paper Piecing Pattern B

Foundation Paper Piecing Pattern A

1

2

3

4

1

2

3

C-7: Double Pinwheel

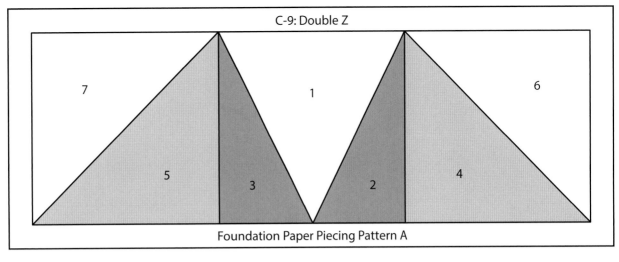

C-9: Double Z

Foundation Paper Piecing Pattern A

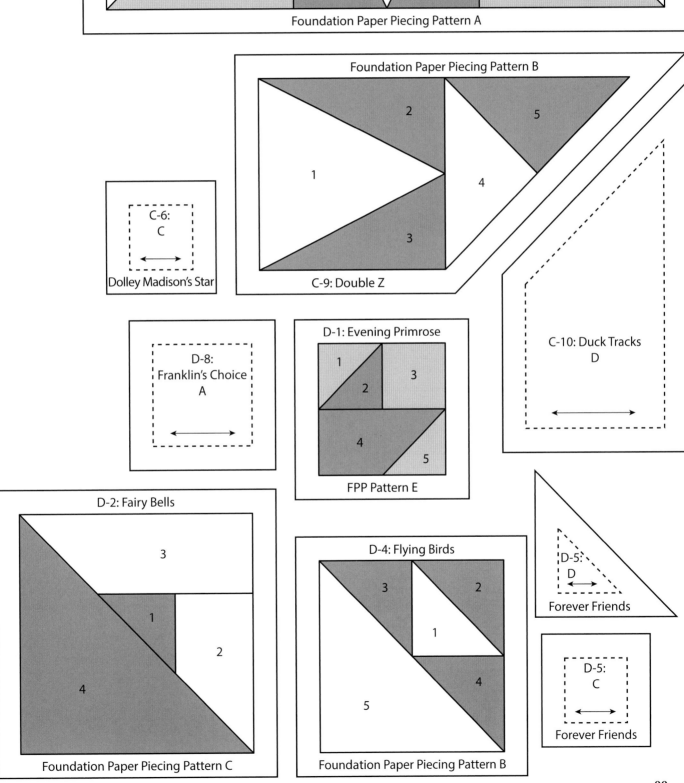

Foundation Paper Piecing Pattern B

C-9: Double Z

C-6:
C

Dolley Madison's Star

D-8:
Franklin's Choice
A

D-1: Evening Primrose

FPP Pattern E

C-10: Duck Tracks
D

D-2: Fairy Bells

Foundation Paper Piecing Pattern C

D-4: Flying Birds

Foundation Paper Piecing Pattern B

D-5:
D

Forever Friends

D-5:
C

Forever Friends

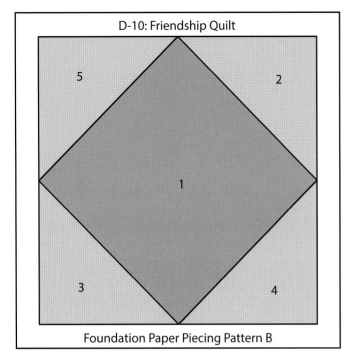

D-10: Friendship Quilt

Foundation Paper Piecing Pattern B

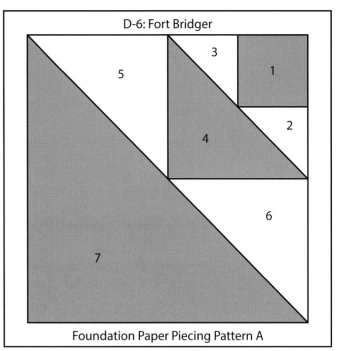

D-6: Fort Bridger

Foundation Paper Piecing Pattern A

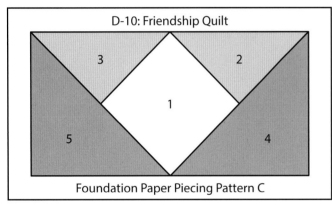

D-10: Friendship Quilt

Foundation Paper Piecing Pattern C

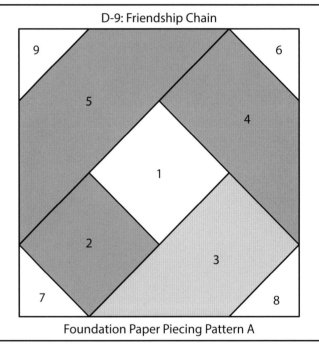

D-9: Friendship Chain

Foundation Paper Piecing Pattern A

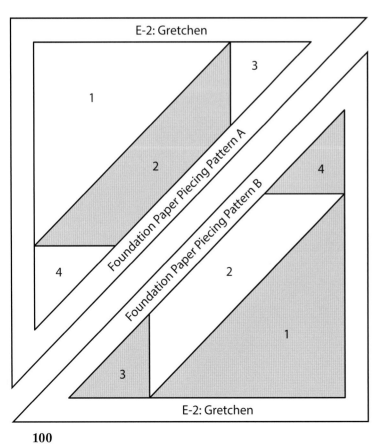

E-2: Gretchen

Foundation Paper Piecing Pattern A

Foundation Paper Piecing Pattern B

E-2: Gretchen

100

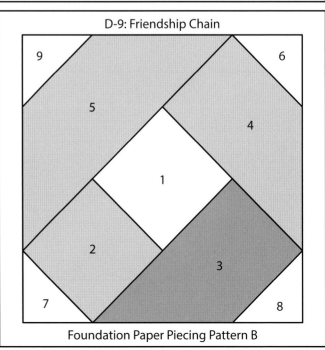

D-9: Friendship Chain

Foundation Paper Piecing Pattern B

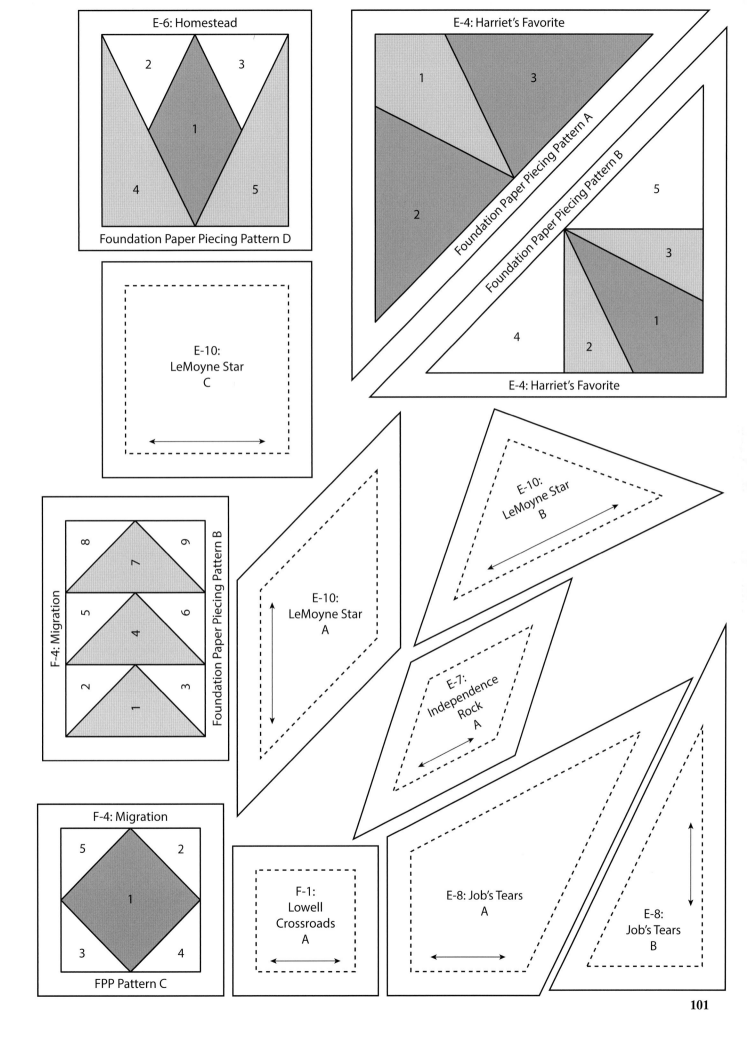

E-6: Homestead

2   3

1

4   5

Foundation Paper Piecing Pattern D

E-4: Harriet's Favorite

1   3

Foundation Paper Piecing Pattern A

Foundation Paper Piecing Pattern B

2

5

3

4   2   1

E-4: Harriet's Favorite

E-10:
LeMoyne Star
C

E-10:
LeMoyne Star
B

F-4: Migration

8   9
7
5   6
4
2   3
1

Foundation Paper Piecing Pattern B

E-10:
LeMoyne Star
A

E-7:
Independence
Rock
A

F-4: Migration

5   2
1
3   4

FPP Pattern C

F-1:
Lowell
Crossroads
A

E-8: Job's Tears
A

E-8:
Job's Tears
B

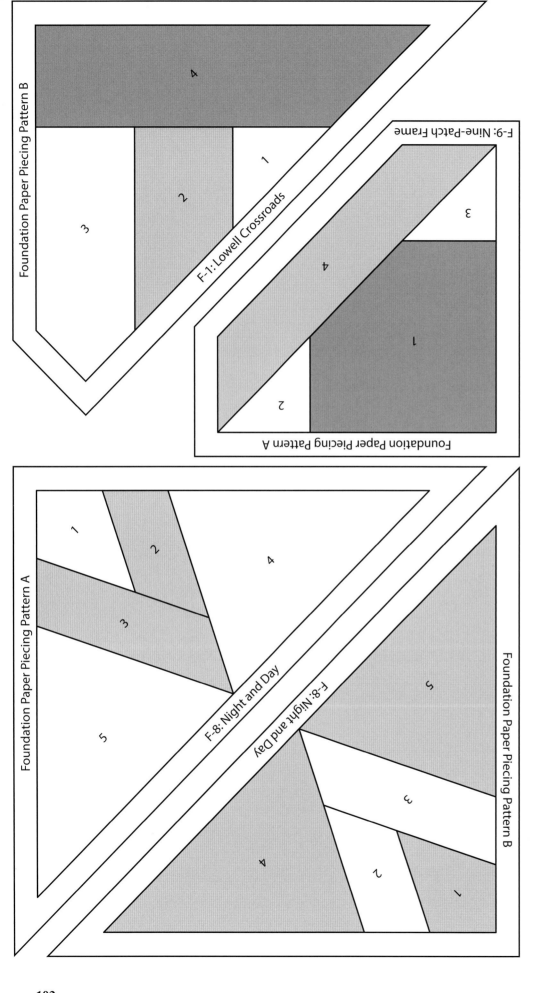

Foundation Paper Piecing Pattern B

F-1: Lowell Crossroads

F-9: Nine-Patch Frame

Foundation Paper Piecing Pattern A

Foundation Paper Piecing Pattern A

F-8: Night and Day

Foundation Paper Piecing Pattern B

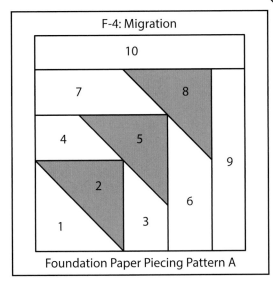

F-4: Migration

Foundation Paper Piecing Pattern A

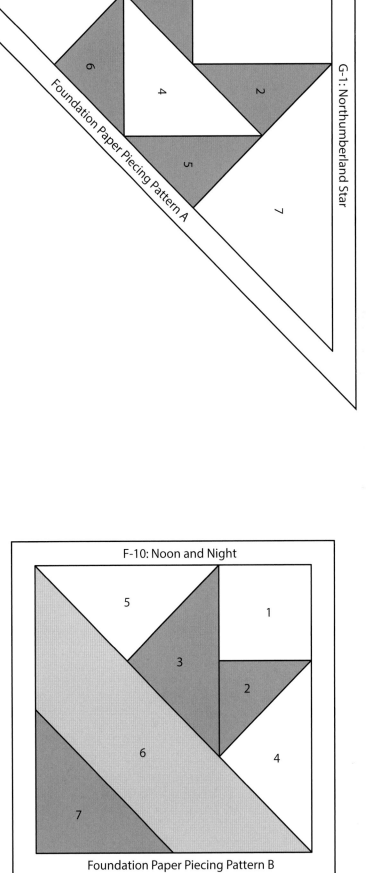

G-1: Northumberland Star

Foundation Paper Piecing Pattern A

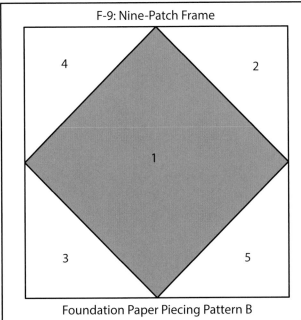

F-9: Nine-Patch Frame

Foundation Paper Piecing Pattern B

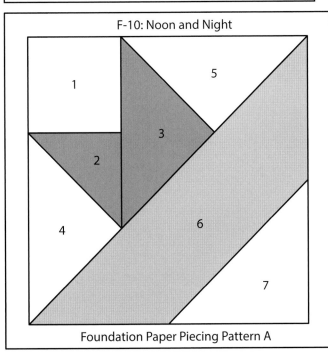

F-10: Noon and Night

Foundation Paper Piecing Pattern A

F-10: Noon and Night

Foundation Paper Piecing Pattern B

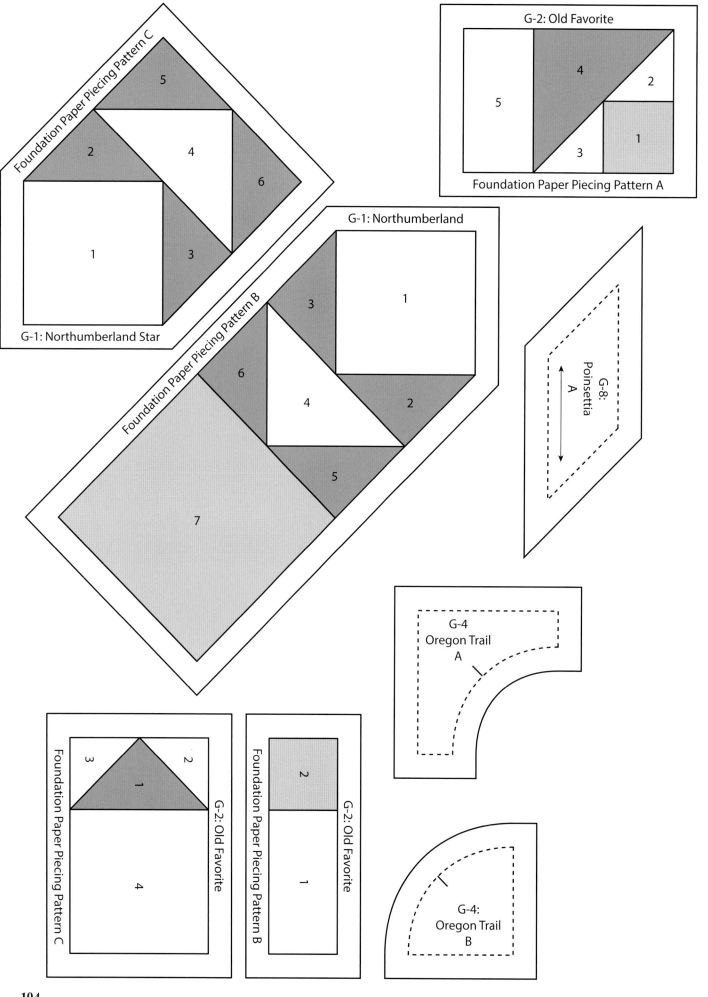

Foundation Paper Piecing Pattern C

G-1: Northumberland Star

G-2: Old Favorite
Foundation Paper Piecing Pattern A

G-1: Northumberland
Foundation Paper Piecing Pattern B

G-8:
Poinsettia
A

G-4
Oregon Trail
A

Foundation Paper Piecing Pattern C
G-2: Old Favorite

Foundation Paper Piecing Pattern B
G-2: Old Favorite

G-4:
Oregon Trail
B

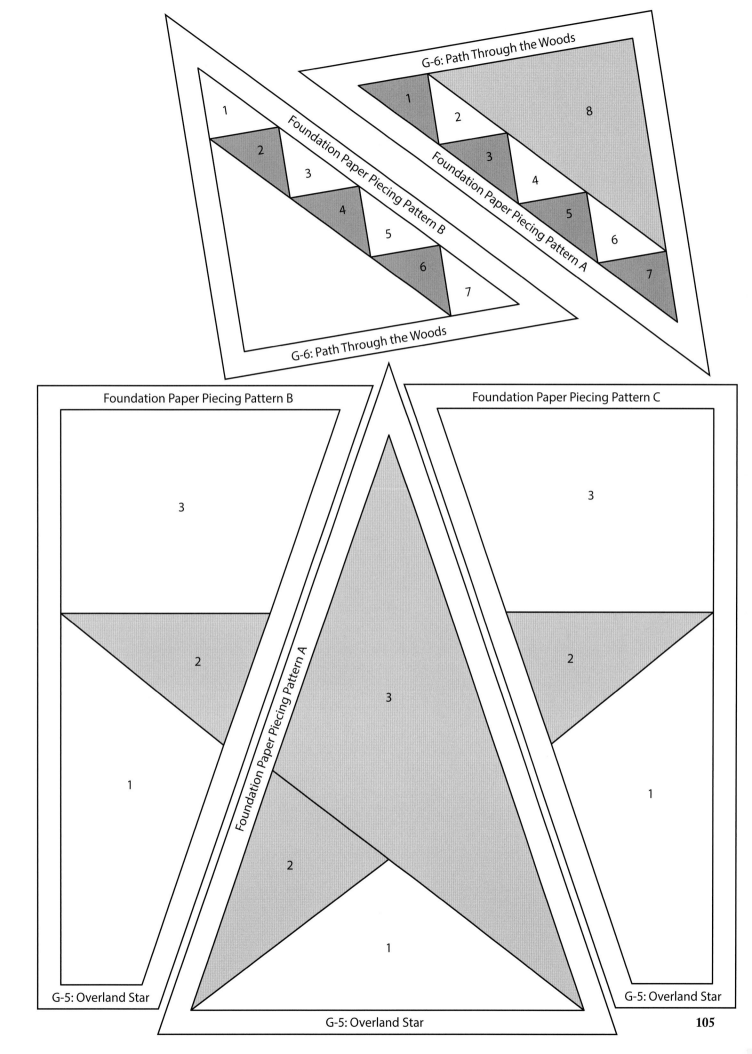

G-6: Path Through the Woods

Foundation Paper Piecing Pattern A

1
2
3
4
5
6
7
8

Foundation Paper Piecing Pattern B

1
2
3
4
5
6
7

G-6: Path Through the Woods

Foundation Paper Piecing Pattern B

Foundation Paper Piecing Pattern C

Foundation Paper Piecing Pattern A

G-5: Overland Star

1
2
3

G-5: Overland Star

G-5: Overland Star

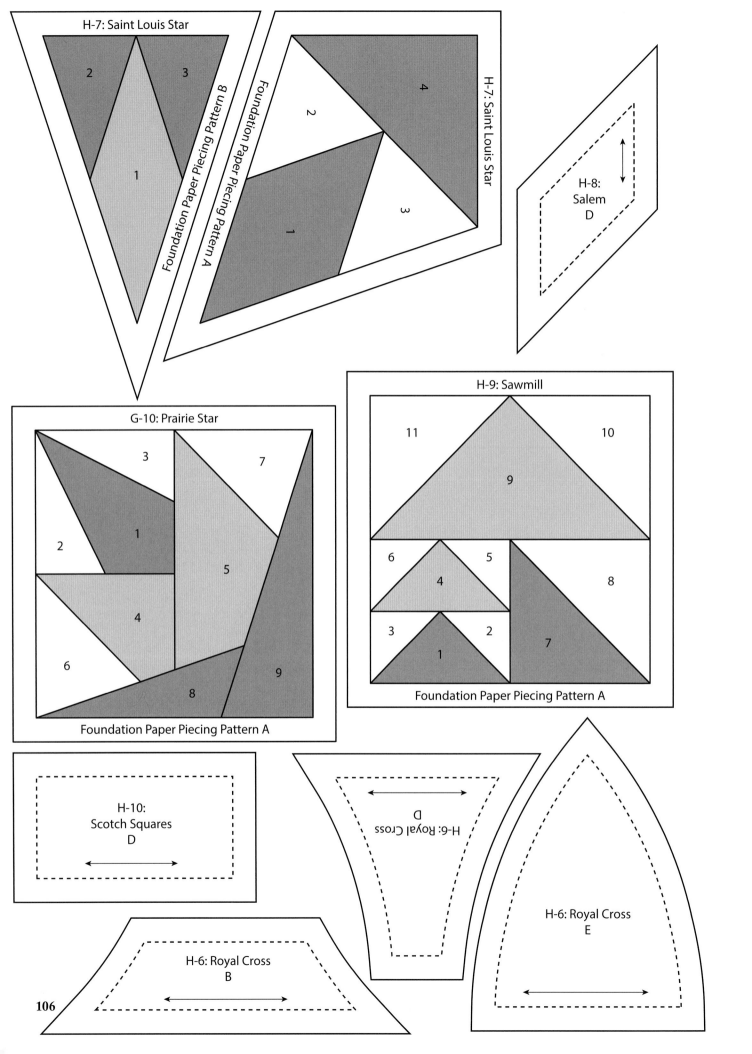

H-7: Saint Louis Star

Foundation Paper Piecing Pattern B

2

3

1

Foundation Paper Piecing Pattern A

2

4

1

3

H-7: Saint Louis Star

H-8: Salem D

H-9: Sawmill

11

10

9

6

5

4

3

1

2

7

8

Foundation Paper Piecing Pattern A

G-10: Prairie Star

3

7

2

1

5

4

6

9

8

Foundation Paper Piecing Pattern A

H-10: Scotch Squares D

H-6: Royal Cross D

H-6: Royal Cross E

H-6: Royal Cross B

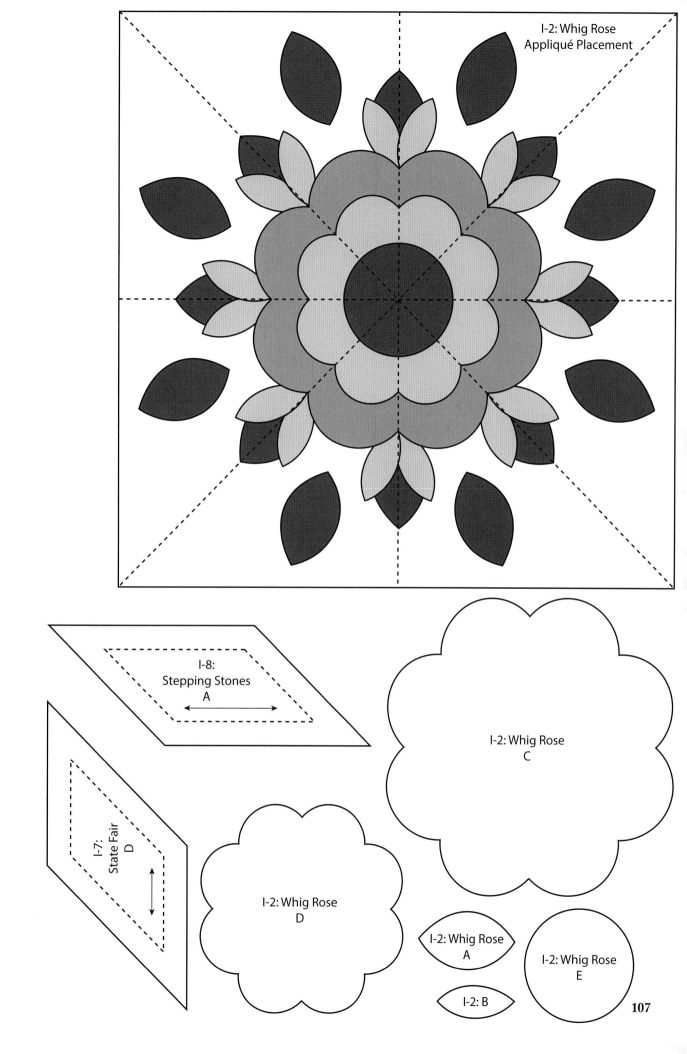

I-2: Whig Rose
Appliqué Placement

I-8:
Stepping Stones
A

I-2: Whig Rose
C

I-7:
State Fair
D

I-2: Whig Rose
D

I-2: Whig Rose
A

I-2: Whig Rose
E

I-2: B

107

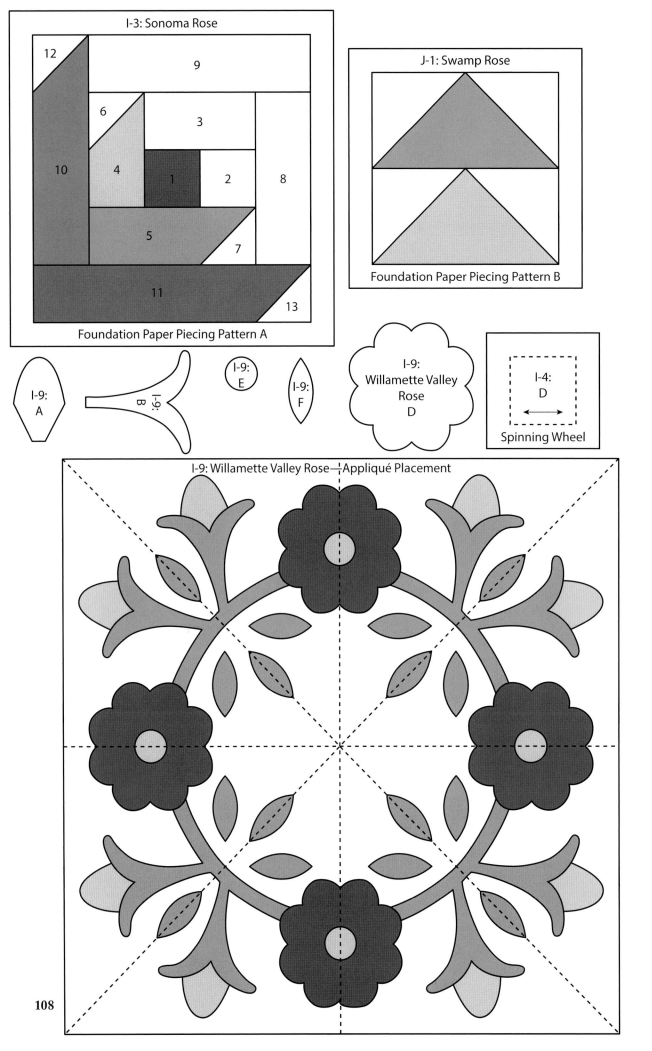

I-3: Sonoma Rose

12 9 6 3 10 4 1 2 8 5 7 11 13

Foundation Paper Piecing Pattern A

J-1: Swamp Rose

Foundation Paper Piecing Pattern B

I-9: A

I-9: B

I-9: E

I-9: F

I-9: Willamette Valley Rose D

I-4: D

Spinning Wheel

I-9: Willamette Valley Rose—Appliqué Placement

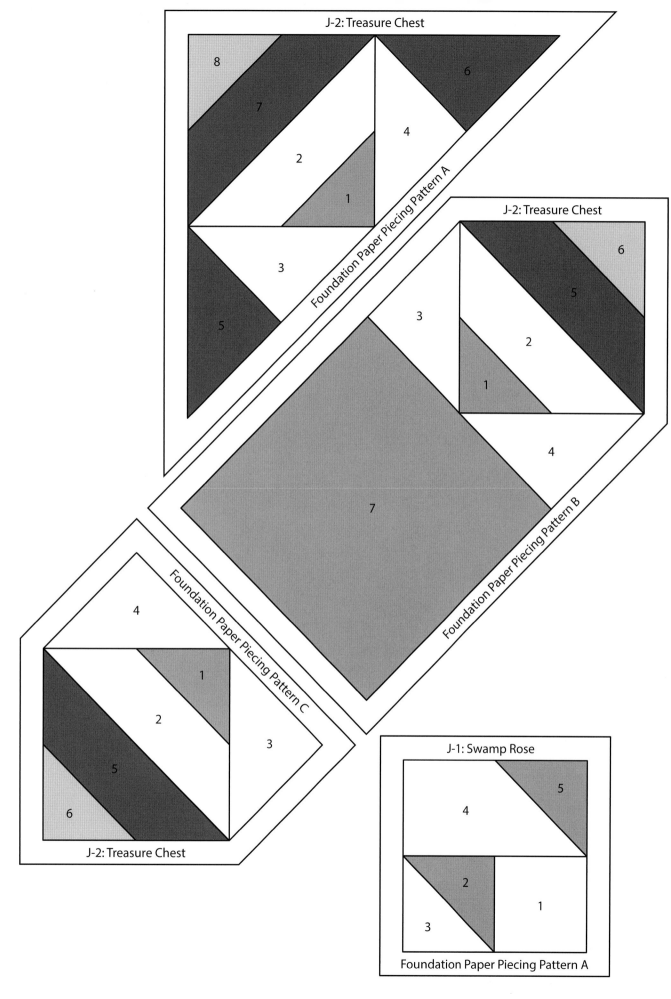

J-2: Treasure Chest

Foundation Paper Piecing Pattern A

J-2: Treasure Chest

Foundation Paper Piecing Pattern B

Foundation Paper Piecing Pattern C

J-2: Treasure Chest

J-1: Swamp Rose

Foundation Paper Piecing Pattern A

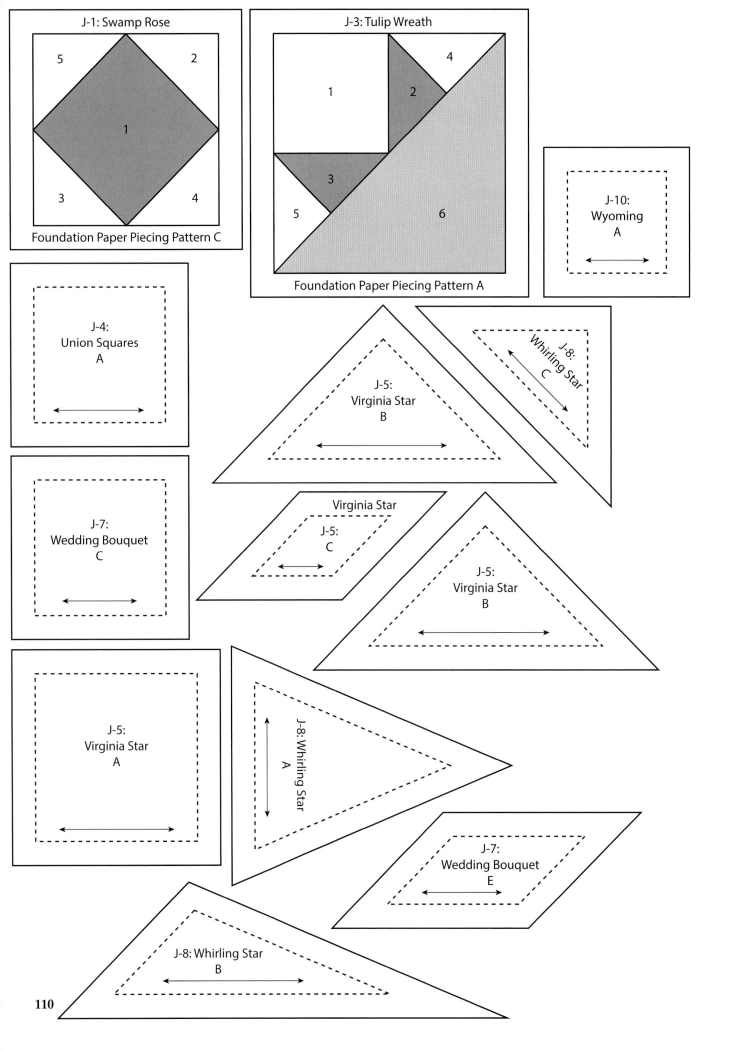

J-1: Swamp Rose

5   2

1

3   4

Foundation Paper Piecing Pattern C

J-3: Tulip Wreath

1   2   4

3

5   6

Foundation Paper Piecing Pattern A

J-10: Wyoming A

J-4: Union Squares A

J-7: Wedding Bouquet C

J-5: Virginia Star A

J-5: Virginia Star B

J-8: Whirling Star C

Virginia Star J-5: C

J-5: Virginia Star B

J-8: Whirling Star A

J-7: Wedding Bouquet E

J-8: Whirling Star B

About the Author

Jennifer Chiaverini is *The New York Times* best-selling author of acclaimed historical novels and the beloved Elm Creek Quilts series, as well as seven collections of quilt patterns from C&T Publishing inspired by her books.

Her original quilt designs have been featured in *Country Woman*; *Quiltmaker*; *Quiltmaker's 100 Blocks, Volumes 3–5*; and *Quilt*; and her short stories have appeared in *Quiltmaker* and *Quilters Newsletter*.

A graduate of the University of Notre Dame and the University of Chicago, she lives with her husband and two sons in Madison, Wisconsin.

About her historical fiction, the *Milwaukee Journal Sentinel* writes, "In addition to simply being fascinating stories, these novels go a long way in capturing the texture of life for women, rich and poor, black and white, in those perilous years."

Visit Jennifer online and follow on social media!

Website: jenniferchiaverini.com • **Facebook:** @JenniferChiaveriniAuthor • **Twitter:** @jchiaverini

Also by Jennifer Chiaverini:

By Jennifer Chiaverini and Nancy Odom:

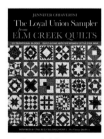

| Available as an eBook and Print-On-Demand only | Available as an eBook only | Available as an eBook and Print-On-Demand only | Available as an eBook only | Available as an eBook only | Available as an eBook and Print-On-Demand only |